ISSUES AND TRENDS
IN CRITICAL PEDAGOGY

Critical Education and Ethics

Editors

Barry Kanpol, *Penn State-Harrisburg*

Fred Yeo, *Southeast Missouri State University*

Issues and Trends in Critical Pedagogy
  Barry Kanpol

Forthcoming

Teachers Talking Back and Breaking Bread
  Barry Kanpol
The Ethics of Critical Pedagogy: The Need for a Moral
  Compact in Educational Reform
  Barry Kanpol and Fred Yeo
Popular Culture in Everyday Life
  Suren Lalvani
Demarcating the Borders of Chicano(a)/Latina(o) Education
  Juan S. Munoz, Carlos Tejada, Corrine Martinez,
  Zeus Leonardo and Peter McLaren
From Otherness to Cultural Democracy
  Suzanne SooHoo
Teaching as a Spirital Activity: A Classroom as a
  Place of Darkness and Mystery
  Carol Zinn

ISSUES AND TRENDS IN CRITICAL PEDAGOGY

BARRY KANPOL
PENN STATE-HARRISBURG

HAMPTON PRESS, INC.
CRESSKILL, NEW JERSEY

Printed in Canada

Library of Congress Cataloging-in-Publication Data

Kanpol, Barry
    Issues and trends in critical pedagogy / Barry Kanpol.
      p. cm. -- (Critical ethics and education)
    Includes bibliographical references and indexes.
    ISBN 1-57273-084-6 (cloth). -- ISBN 1-57273-085-4 (pbk.)
    1. Critical pedagogy. I. Title. II. Series.
LC196.K368 1996
370.115--dc20
                                         96-44099
                                             CIP

Hampton Press, Inc.
23 Broadway
Cresskill, NJ 07626

*To all teachers who are struggling for
a "critical" space in their lives*

CONTENTS

SERIES FOREWORD

As we contemplate the rapidly approaching 21st century, with its promises of new technologies, cyber-realities, new subjectivities, and cultural demands for new responses to old transcendent questions, American schooling is increasingly defined by arthritic traditionalisms of standardized assessment and testing, school and teacher accountabilities, models of exacerbated efficiency and tracking, and ever more strident state and federal calls for more of the same. The lack of vision in and out of the American educational establishment continues to underwrite the spread of the "savage inequalities" that Kozol (1991) found so disparaging in inner-city schools, even to those in hitherto secluded suburbia. Mired in their increasingly narrow traditional practices and corporate market logic, American schools and their government factotums trumpet national reports that herald increasing failure and simultaneously increasing reliance on syllogisms that wipe away democratic and humanistic possibilities. American education faces the potentialities of the future with the instruments of the past.

With the above in mind, it is no small claim to make that American schooling is representative and simultaneously constitutive of the race, class, and gender disparities illustrative and symptomatic of the larger American society. As an ideologic alternative to both the Mainstream's and Right's configurations of education and society, Critical Theory and its practitioners have long argued that for schools to thrive and be more democratic, inroads must be made to challenge the overt and hidden assumptions that frame American education. Critical theorists argue that we live in an age in which there is an illusion of education and the actuality of profound democratic decline (McLaren, 1991). Progressive multiculturalists such as Banks (1991) and critical multiculturalists such as Nieto (1995), Giroux (1992), and Sleeter and McLaren (1995) have attempted theoretically to identify a critical and politically just pedagogy framed within postmodern understandings of difference and borders of cultural identity to challenge dominant forms of alienation, oppression. and marginalization.

Critical theory has, however, its own contradictions and failures. Although challenging theoretically dominant social, cultural, and educational paradigms, these authors' insights have sadly effected little societal transformation on the way out of the growing despair of poverty, the melanoma of racism (West, 1993), and the general malaise that attends a social system characterized as misanthropic and segregated by class, race, and gender. Critical theorists argue vociferously for American schools to secure a more democratic and egalitarian community; however, they rarely speak in a unified fashion to effect a program for social and/or political change and are seemingly at a loss for answers as to "how to fix things up." Mired in the postmodern quandary, they do not want to be labeled as technocratic strategists, essentialists, and/or pragmatics, so they offer no clear plan or normative framework to guide the changes they advocate. In many senses, despite the validity of their critique, critical theorists have become stymied by an intolerance of praxis.

The foregoing, as a pedagogically theoretical, practical, and professional realization, has prompted us and others (e.g., Purpel & Shapiro, 1995) to view what has become known as the postmodernist critique with increasing cynicism and a growing concern that the questions that we are asking may well be the wrong ones. The influences of postmodernism on critical theory, although insightful, have acted to splinter transformative possibilities resulting in a dizzying array of balkanized positions and interpretations among radical educational theorists. Yet, what would represent a unifying possibility for the current disarray of the Left, a "politics of meaning" for education?

In response, and central to our purpose, a few theorists on the Left, notably those grounded in some form of liberation theology or holism, have argued that crises of both the Mainstream and the Left are not just political or economic but are at their heart moral and spiritual. Specifically, Cornel West argues that the need for change is fueled by what he terms a "human quest"—a reconceptualization of the democratic and ethical implications of a spiritual conception of what it is to be human (West, 1993) in an era often labeled as being represented by a failure of conscience. While the political Left has powerfully argued about the demise of political democracy and social equity (Giroux, 1992; McLaren, 1991) and education's place in that, others have critiqued the Left for its cynicism and nihilism (Habermas, 1987; Purpel & Shapiro, 1995; West, 1993). We argue that the Left's ineffectualness is due to a failure to ground political critique in moral possibility. In our opinion, the struggle of the academic educational Left, particularly one that is rooted within the postmodern, is bereft of the language of the ethical or the moral—the human language of hope which must frame any obscure discourse of change, possibility, and justice. The educational Mainstream and Right have forgotten that democracy is about change, and the Left has failed to understand that it is also about hope, the moral, and the spiritual—what some have termed as *prophetic education*.

Instead of writing about an agenda of commitment to community, the Left, conforming to a postmodern sensibility, has parlayed—one might suggest even trapped—itself into fragmentation; a politics of division, exclusion, separation, and irrelevance. The critical endeavor has become an end in itself, and in our sentiment lacks the moral and ethical certitude of commitment to a humane and democratic vision of social justice based on a notion of human compassion, hope, and even spirituality—all of which form the foundation of human imagining that life can be better, fairer, more just.

Although we acknowledge that this argument has and is being asserted in education by a few critical theorists, it is either framed within generalized social concerns or is targeted at mainstream suburban schools. Even the most trenchant of arguments posed by the Left are aimed at general education, often reifying the social in a political critique. Lost amidst this discussion are those schools most in need of transformative possibilities—urban and inner-city school sites and their attendant communities. Admittedly, critical theorists and researchers in education have attempted some description and theorizing on the systemics and dehumanization of inner-city education; on the need to reconstruct both the social and ideologic paradigms of how we understand education in general; and on the need to incorporate educationally configured postmodern understandings of issues such as difference, identity, ethnicity, race, gender, marginalization, the `other', and so on.

Yet, it seems to us that each of these still misses being able to mobilize, to stir, and to motivate their respective audience and the greater public to effect change. In some cases, these writers have unintentionally obfuscated potential practical frameworks for transformative change within the esoterica of theory. In others, although advocating social transformation, the practicalities of effecting such change in schools has been lost within an essentially political menu. It is our argument that in order to effect a redemocratization of the social and the educational in this country, a fusion or synthesis must occur among insights offered by critical theory, postmodernism, and liberation spiritualism. More specifically, we believe the response to the issue of balkanization and/or the irrelevance caused by theories of fractionalization to be to ask and address the heretofore unasked questions; that is, to seek possibilities for radical transformation within a moral and spiritual framework in which a critical argument is subsumed in an ethical one. Put differently, it is time for critical theorists and pedagogists to pose the eminently practical and ultimately ethical question of what constitutes the "good society."

With the above in mind, our aim and purpose in this series is to bridge the gap between the educational Left, as embodied within postmodern criticality, and the prophetic or spiritual tradition within all its multiplicities. This series is derived from a concern for a morally and spiritually driven vision that has to date been severely underplayed in, if not outright missing from, the literature of educational critique and thereby left to the religious Right to parlay its truncated orthodoxy into the nation's political, educational, and social discourse. Within this series, we propose to provide a forum to investigate the parameters of a morally grounded prophetic and democratic platform intended to fulfill the critical theorists' ideas of the possibilities of educational and social change in general; change that must be morally, ethically, and spiritually grounded in a transcendent and subjective critique, hope, and humanity.

Barry Kanpol
Penn State University-Harrisburg

Fred Yeo
Southeast Missouri State University

REFERENCES

Banks, J.A. (1991). *Teaching strategies for ethnic studies* (5th ed.). Boston: Allyn and Bacon.

Giroux, H. (1992). *Border crossings: Cultural workers and the politics of education*. New York: Routledge.

Habermas, J. (1987). *The philosophic discourse of modernity*. Cambridge, MA: MIT Press.

Kozol, J. (1991). *Savage inequalities: Children in America's schools*. New York: Crown.

McLaren, P. (1991). Critical pedagogy: Constructing an arch of social dreaming and a doorway to hope. *Journal of Education, 173*(1).

Nieto, S. (1995) Affirming diversity: The sociopolitical context of multicultural education (2nd ed.). New York: Longman.

Purpel, D. & Shapiro, S. (1995). *Beyond liberation and excellence: Towards a new public discourse for education*. New York: Routledge.

Sleeter, C., & McLaren P. (Eds.). (1995). *Multicultural education, critical pedagogy and the politics of discourse*. Albany: SUNY Press.

West, C. (1993). *Race matters*. Boston: Beacon Press.

EDITOR'S PREFACE: CRITICAL PEDAGOGY WITHIN CLASSROOM PRACTICES

As we approach the end of the 20th century and after several decades of critique and counter-proposal by educational theorists and practitioners from the radical left, the nation's schools continue to be noted for their emphasis on standardized testing, accountability models framed in a Social Darwinist language of efficiency and excellence, hierarchal tracking schemes, increasing rates of failure, and disintegrating resource bases. We seem to live within a political, economic, and social climate that exacerbates an illusion of education in an age of democratic decline (McLaren, 1991). Mainstream educators and reformers seemingly can find no way out of the current educational crisis except to issue calls for more of the same, and the Left critique has become increasingly balkanized and splintered under the baleful influence of postmodern notions of incommensurable and irreconcilable differences. Diversity and vast cultural and demographic ranges of human difference are rapidly becoming the norm in even suburban schools, yet educational systems have yet to come to terms with the needs of people of color and/or class. In fact, it can be argued that American education both as institution and social system has opted to actively deflect notions of difference and social critique in favor of stringent advocacy of assimilation, marginalization, and failure. Increasingly, the nation has begun to construct a web of laws, economies, and education systemics to delegitimate and demonize diversity.

Education continues to rely on rationales grounded in 19th-century notions of assimilation to justify late 20th-century practices that deny both culture and identity for students and teachers of color. In a period when demographic change is gaining momentum and students are increasingly non-white and/or non-English speaking, teacher education continues to seek its prospects from young, white, rural, or suburban females, and adopt assimilationist, deculturalizing methods of intervention into families and social aggregates that belie the American Dream. It is clear that the political and social "conversation" in this country is framed by a national compact delineated by profound tensions and represented by a racialized ideology, a misanthropic sense of gender, including deep homophobia, and fear of poverty and difference. In this mix, the Left critique is all but silent as conservative and/or corporate rhetoric captures increasingly the ideologies and practices that constitute our national notions of education.

The Left has, however, not been inactive throughout this period. In a virtual cornucopia of writings, texts, treatises, and articles it has attempted to construct a critique calling attention to the nondemocratic nature of American education and its capture by corporate and Right interests; to argue for the importance of demystifying difference, identity and cultural borders, and the need to unmask the dangers of ethnicity theory; and to challenge dominant American sociocultural forms of alienation, oppression, and marginalization. Although the Left critique has written extensively about the demise of democracy and hope, particularly within education, argued strenuously for the reconstruction of social justice and equality within this country, and theorized on the effects of popular culture, it has also increasingly conformed to a postmodern sensibility set often in a hypertextualized format that is unreachable to educational practitioners. The Left has parleyed itself into political fragmentation while decrying the rationales for collective commitment, thus leaving only a politics of division, exclusion, and separation (Purpel & Shapiro, 1995). The critical endeavor has seemingly become caught in a vicious circle of deconstruction, lacking the certitude to proffer the practical vision of democracy and justice it desires. The question of practicalizing that critique and harnessing its interrogative power within the praxis of classrooms and schools is the aim of Kanpol's text, *Issues and Trends in Critical Pedagogy*.

Here, Kanpol describes and analyzes critical theorists' notions about education becoming an arena for the struggle for social change, specifically that variant of Critical Theory that is framed by postmodern understandings of difference, identity, intersubjectivity and denial of position within which much of the modern metanarrative has been grounded. In a series of chapters, some drawn from other sympathetic authors, some analytic, others narrative based, Kanpol extends his arguments and proposals from a previous effort to place critical pedagogy within the reach of school-based educators (Kanpol, 1994). In this book, he again acknowledges and espouses the theoretical understandings that critical theorists of all varieties have produced. However, he advocates the loosening of the grip of higher academia on the promulgation of Critical Pedagogy to allow for its translation into intelligible praxis by teachers and administrators.

Through the inclusion of a series of what may seem to be diverse chapters, Kanpol sketches a central theme that argues that the postmodern critical theorists posit a transformational argument rarely accessible to educational practitioners, but one that has broad potentialities for social and educational change if adopted by educational practitioners. As Maxine Greene noted in a review of another Kanpol text (1993), what is needed is to make clear the impact of power on curricular privileging, and that is what this text intends, but it does so arguably at a level graspable by the teachers and administrators on whom actualization will depend. It openly advocates a form of critical pragmatism aimed at introducing teachers to a more emancipatory pedagogical potential, albeit understanding that such potential is and will be muted by the very ideological and cultural constraints that critical pedagogy interrogates and disputes.

It is the intent of this series, Critical Education and Ethics, to promote dialog and conversation grounded in the critical approach, mediated by postmodern, feminist, and multiculturalist concerns and theory, and to move and open the discussion into venues that postmodernist critical pedagogy has not gone. In this text, Barry Kanpol offers a grasp on the educational everyday but insists that it be interpreted from within a critical perspective so as to open up the silences of mainstream education. It is a text about schools and schooling that attempts translation of emancipatory theory to the schoolroom, while arguing for the interpretation of the structure and processes of the latter within the multifariousness of critical dreams of possibility. Whether arguable or not, the text adds to our understanding of education in this country, but also offers possibilities for practical transformation of that same system.

Fred Yeo, Editor
Southeast Missouri State University

REFERENCES

Greene, M. (1993, June). Review essay: Reflections on postmodernism and education, *Educational Policy, 7*(2), 206-211.

Kanpol, B. (1994). *Critical pedagogy: An introduction.* Westport, CT:
    Bergin & Garvey.
McLaren, P. (1991). Critical pedagogy: Constructing an arch of social
    dreaming and a doorway to hope. *Journal of Education, 173*(1).
Purpel, D., & Shapiro, S. (1995). *Beyond liberation and excellence:
    Towards a new public discourse for education.* New York:
    Routledge.

ACKNOWLEDGMENTS

No book is written without the help of others. For that reason I am particularly grateful to my students (in- and pre-service) who have both challenged critical pedagogical ideas and made me rethink the limitations and possibilities of critical pedagogy. I am thankful to Fred Yeo for his critical insights. And, at the time this book was constructed, my wife Susan was selfless in creating extra time for me. Of course, having three children always reminds me of what comes first in life. It is to Merav, Maia, and Christopher that I indeed owe thanks.

PERMISSIONS

Several chapters in this volume are substantially revised versions of previously published material. Permission has been granted for the following chapters:

Chapter 3: The concept of "resistance": Further scrutiny. *Critical Pedagogy Networker, 2*(1), 1989. Geelong, Australia: Deakin University.

Chapter 4: Critical pedagogy and the multicultural project. *Critical Pedagogy Networker, 7*(2-3). Adelaide, Australia: Flinders University.

Chapter 5: A contradiction of teacher professionalism.: A gender critique. *Critical Pedagogy Networker, 3*(4), 1990. Geelong, Australia: Deakin University.

Chapter 6: A critical pedagogy for principals: Necessary conditions for moral leadership. *Australian Administrator, 12*(4), 1991. Geelong, Australia: Deakin University.

Chapter 8: Review of Henry Giroux's *Disturbing Pleasure: Learning Popular Culture. Educational Studies, 26*(4), 345-352, 1995.

Chapter 9: Outcome-based education and democratic commitment: Hopes and possibilities. *Educational Policy, 9*(4), 359-374. © 1995 Corwin Press, Inc.

Chapter 10: Critical pedagogy and liberation theology: Borders for a transformative agenda. *Educational Theory, 16*(1), 105-117, 1996.

PART I

THE DEVELOPMENT OF CRITICAL PEDAGOGY

THE CONTINUING RESURGENCE OF CRITICAL PEDAGOGY

> Equally important is the necessity for teachers and other educators
> to reject educational theories that reduce schooling either to the
> domain of learning theory or to forms of technocratic rationality that
> ignore the central concerns of social change, power relations, and
> conflicts both within and outside of schools. (Giroux, 1983, p. 62)

The urgency of this quote from prominent critical theorist in
education, Henry Giroux, from as far back as in 1983, is *still* in effect
today. The debates around school reform and what constitutes a
"good" education are ever persistent. Furthermore, as we approach
the 21st century, these debates are furiously ongoing[1] despite their
inadequacy of viewing schools, as stated earlier, as sites of conflict
and disharmony.

---

[1]Over the last 15 years or so there have been a number of national reports
such as the National Commission on Excellence in Education (1983),
(Washington, D.C.: U.S. Government Printing Office) translated into "A
Nation at Risk: An Imperative for Educational Reform" (1983). For a
comprehensive summary of this report, see Shapiro (1985) (see also Apple's
[1983] critique, especially chapter 5, as well as the 1986, Carnegie Report,
and more recently over the last few years, Outcomes Based Education). For
critiques on Outcomes Based Education, see Kanpol (1995b), Capper and
Jamison (1993), and McQuaide and Pliska (1993).

With this in mind we live in times of increasing uncertainty as to how to "fix" up the public education arena, described by Kozol (1991) as exacerbating "savage inequalities." To *fix up* is an ambiguous term to use at best. The fixing up will depend on who is in power, who has control, and who makes decisions, particularly regarding the education domain that this book deals with. Ultimately, to fix up has a political bent because it largely depends on deeply held values and beliefs—by those who are repairing, so to speak! To fix up also implies there is a problem that needs serious attention. In part, this is where critical pedagogy fuels many of its initial arguments.

In a recent book of mine, *Critical Pedagogy: An Introduction* (1994), the primary intent was to focus on language and ideas accessible to the general public and everyday teacher, and to outline the possibilities that critical pedagogy holds to challenge the ever-present and ongoing alienation, subordination, and oppression of various peoples, in particular teachers and students. This work introduced the beginning social activist teacher, both theoretically and practically, to limitations and possibilities of social consciousness raising within curricular and other realistic structural constraints.

It is no small feat, it was argued, that teachers challenge state-mandated curricular within alternative meaning-making systems, attempt to abolish both their own and others' stereotypes, compete fairly so that all students can have a chance at success, and redefine teacher and student authority. The list of challenges that teachers face to end various forms of inequities is neverending.[2]

Critical pedagogy, both within its philosophical realm and through its practical import, has been an extremely important but highly underused, underrepresented, and misunderstood response to the present general morbid conditions of our public schools. Touted as radical or extreme in its political position, an argument in my *Introduction* (1994) book was simply that in mission and goals critical pedagogy was and still is democratic in intent, yet extremely critical when democracy is thwarted. Critical pedagogy, at its most critical, is highly skeptical of a society that can allow "savage inequalities" to occur as Kozol (1991, 1994) reminds us so well; is highly charged against sexual-, race-, and class-based aberrations; and is equally passionate about positioning both teachers and students (for our case in this book) as well as administrators, such as principals and the like, in places where they can be the creators of

---

[2]Throughout this book I use the term "deskilling" to signify a teacher's *lack of control* over their personal and professional lives at the school site.

their own meaning-making systems—systems that in fact both undercut experiences of oppression, alienation, and subordination and transform these experiences into joyful expressions of fair and just social relations.

As a follow-up to the *Introduction*, this work's basic presupposition is that there are indeed many facets to the growing critical pedagogical tradition, much of which has been written about in opaque forms and unfortunately little of which has been written in a straightforward and down-to-earth language that the layperson can read. Thus, this book attempts to share with readers in what I hope will be accessible language the fruits of others' labors, as well as my own. I borrow from tradition, historically constructed, in which various elements of critical pedagogy have been written, the seeds of which lie in the towering figures of John Dewey, George Counts, and presently Paulo Freire, Henry Giroux, and Maxine Greene, along with countless others such as Michael Apple and Peter McLaren, who all have responded so nobly to the nightmarish conditions of our schools. Also, critical pedagogy is *not* only a "white" person's response to the present morbid public school conditions. Critical pedagogues arise from different traditions and heritages, both in and out of the educational arena. Cornel West (1982, 1993), bell hooks (1994, 1989), Antonio Darder (1991), Sonia Nieto (1996), and the like can attest to this.

To me, anyway, as I know to many other critical pedagogues, critical pedagogy is not just about one or two issues. It is not just about urban schools, but about suburban and rural schools too. Within these schools, critical pedagogy must be viewed as multidimensional. Critical pedagogical areas of concern could have anything to do with schooling and the wider culture. For instance: What is the relationship of critical pedagogy to multiculturalism, to gender, to race, to principals, to literacy, to professionalism, to leadership, to educational reform, to popular culture, and even to spirituality, which among many other facets of life must guide the explanations and interpretations of the criticalist. My hope in this volume is to present the compelling need for both potential and current teachers as well as the general public to understand the basic components of critical pedagogy and where their essential elements may lie, particularly as related to our schools and the wider culture. Ultimately, critical pedagogy *must* be taken seriously as a public movement rather than just jargon used only within academic elitist circles.

A LITTLE HISTORY

Perhaps a good place to continue this opening chapter is around the Industrial Revolution era, or the beginning of what theorists both in and out of the education field of knowledge call *modernity*, approximately the 1850s and beyond. Education was typically for the upper class and male privileged at that time and was also a necessary condition for a growing society preparing citizens for economic survival and ultimate national prosperity. Mass education was a turning point in American history, especially as it was in some ways related to mass immigration. Women were demanding the right for access to knowledge (a right for education), and concurrently there was a dire need to produce functional workers to meet economic needs.

By the 20th century there was no option but to build a school system that would be effective in mastery, prediction, and control. Put another way, one method to galvanize the masses through education was simply to develop what was to become known as the *social efficiency* system, a by-product of a growing industrialized and bureaucratized society. Simply put, "social efficiency" became an ideological construct in which schools became productive sites run much like a factory model. This was in full force in American schools (and businesses) by the 1920s. As Spring (1993) says:

> Social efficiency thinking mandated that workers be scientifically selected and trained for their particular jobs and that cooperation between management and workers occur so as to insure all of the work being done in accordance with principles of the sciences has been developed. The principles of hierarchical management, scientific study and control of the elements in the organization, selection and training of individuals for places within the organization, and cost-effectiveness became the focus for the professionalization of public school administration. (p. 256)

This resulted in school administrators keeping true to these roles and thus trying to establish standardized procedures. Spring comments further:

> Standardization became the magic word. Administrators were preoccupied with standardizing student forms, evaluations of teachers and students, attendance records, personnel records, and hiring procedures. Cost-effectiveness also became an important part of this process as administrators worried about cost-effectiveness in the classrooms, the ordering of supplies, the purchase of insurance, building maintenance, and the office management. (p. 257)

Ultimately the social efficiency system meant standardizing time, space, curriculum, pedagogy, jobs, and the like. Resultantly, with the onset of tracking—a highly competitive market logic—the development of social stereotypes, and with school districts often divided along suburban and/or urban lines, schools in general also became sorting machines (Spring, 1989, 1994), bent on institutionalized tracking (Oakes, 1985), and a division of pupils into social classes (Anyon, 1980) in which the economy and economic ideology subverted any democratic intent that schools were touted to have (Bowles & Gintis, 1976; Shapiro, 1990). Curriculum was ideologically loaded (Anyon, 1979), and education under the guise of social efficiency became the child of an economic pecking order in which this ideology was espoused through hidden and at times manipulative ways (Apple, 1982).

There is no doubt that this pervasive conservative view of schools was challenged by the more progressive forces represented particularly by the likes of John Dewey. As the father of progressive education, particularly in the United States, Dewey was well aware how schools, through their need to produce functioning citizens, were in fact robbing students and the public of an educated citizenry, whose civic function was also to be part of a democratic society. A slew of books and articles by Dewey connecting education to experience (1938), education to democracy (1916), the child to curriculum (1902a), and school to society (1902b), among many others basically challenged traditional education and old individualism (Dewey, 1929) to revamp itself into a new form of democratic hope and possibility.

Schools for Dewey were sites of democratic possibilities, where children, using their experiences and where schools, basing curriculum on experiences, became the continuing democratic experience. This was a moral imperative for Dewey (1909). Schools had to represent the student, *not* detached bits of information forever to be forgotten after the next quiz or test. What seems rather simple to me and I hope to readers—to make schools meaningful places where children can reflect on their experiences as related to curriculum and the world outside of schools—believe it or not was in direct opposition to a social efficiency movement which was based primarily on a market logic and a division of schools that has tragically led to race, class, and gender disparities. Of course, the argument can be made that any school preparing the child for a job is the ultimate responsibility of a working democracy. It would be foolish to disagree with a part of this statement. However, lost over the years within a socially efficient ideological terrain is the equally important task of schools—to prepare students to be morally uprightious, reflective, and critical citizens in a flourishing democracy, a participant in decision making, a part owner of the power and control structures of our society—not just to face life as a robotic worker and consumers!

Many readers would argue that in fact schools have done a good job in preparing students to become productive citizens. However, I remind readers of the savage inequalities within our society (Kozol, 1991) in which the illiteracy rate is rampant, the division of who gets an education as opposed to who does not is racially connected, in which teenagers even in suburbs are seen to commit suicide over their perceived meaningless lives (Gaines, 1992), and in which inner-city youth have little to fight for in terms of receiving a good education (McCall, 1994). Dewey's vision of education did not include staggering illiteracy rates, as well as race, class and gender inequities. Education for Dewey (1939) was for "freedom" not for social disparity, helplessness, despair, alienation, subordination, and oppression.

What is staggering to note is that today Dewey is both felt, understood, accepted and revered by most educators, both conservative and progressive in and out of the academe and public schools. Although progressive, even radical for his times, Dewey today is still just another name that all educators know, but whose language of reflection, experience, democracy, and so on has been co-opted to mean economic freedom and competition for goods and services (represented in schools by grades and high standardized test scores, etc.), all of which supposedly lead to a better standard of living. American education in general has equated Dewey with an *uncritical* form of reflection and experience, a *nonunderstanding* of the importance of Dewey as a social philosopher, whose educational philosophy opposed the dominant American education movement (for the most part, social efficiency) of his and these present unsettling times.

THE RISE OF THE FRANKFURT SCHOOL

Around the time of Dewey's prominence there arose what many theorists particularly outside of education have written about—the German Frankfurt school. Within this school of thought, social critique was the guiding norm. Basically, this critique, led by such philosophers as Walter Benjamin, Herbert Marcuse, Max Horkheimer, and Theodore Adorno, as well as more recently by Jurgen Habermas, have argued that the social world we live in has not been true to enlightenment ideals of democracy and an active and critical citizenry.

As a part of the modern culture, what has replaced these enlightened ideals, they have variously argued, is a market logic of capitalism. Here, scientific management (or Taylorism in the psychology area), "positivism," or "technocratic rationality" has produced a sterile form of thinking or, as Marcuse puts it, "a one-dimensional man." By that he means the structure of repressed personalities are dominated by the social and ideological forces in which man has little or no control. Rather than view the social as dialectical, that is, a fusion of opposites as a point of conflict and possibility to move away from sterile forms of thought, public schools have continued to mirror what the Frankfurt school of thought critiqued.

Although Dewey passed away before much of the initial work of the Frankfurt school was published, he would have agreed with many of their theoretical insights. Like the Frankfurt school, Dewey would have supported the notion of understanding, reflecting, and acting on "experience" as fundamental to shifting consciousness to a higher level, to challenge various forms of oppression, alienation, and subordination. Dewey would have agreed with the Frankfurt school premise of social critique of sterile forms of technocratic thinking— all of which it could possibly be argued led to both the Gulag and the gas chambers of Auschwitz. Dewey would have agreed with a Frankfurt school premise that we live in a society that has at its roots both evil and good, in which the good is a struggle for critical reflection and an active citizenry, and in which the evil that propels social ills must be constantly critiqued and through personal experience and reflection can be both challenged and transformed. In its *worst* sense, Dewey would agree that evil is about *schooling* our students into sterile, uncritical thinkers who accept knowledge at face value, even if that knowledge is problematic. *Education* for Dewey, as I would argue for the Frankfurt school, would be to develop a critical consciousness lacing change and reform with democratic intent, both in theory and in practice.

In "critical" circles of education, such as the one that I am coming out of, there is little direct connection made between the Frankfurt school and John Dewey. I use their connection to derive an historical understanding, construction, and meaning making that defines radical and/or critical pedagogy (otherwise known as critical theory) as a movement that has been historically constructed to challenge the sterile forms of social efficiency that has been a part of what I alluded to earlier as modernism.

With this in mind, there is a need to clarify what has become known in and out of philosophical circles, first in the academe and now in the general public, as both modernism and postmodernism. Although the remainder of this book does not necessarily ground theory and practice in these constructs, for the more theoretical reader there will certainly be moments when either modernism or postmodernism can be applied to the various elements of the following chapters.

Modernism (particularly postindustrialism) is divided into two areas. First, modernism is about individuals struggling toward such goals as freedom and universal peace. Within the enlightenment era and beyond, modernism stresses individual free and critical thinking, social responsibility, reason, rationality, and scientific progress and change. Power, it is argued, is placed in the hands of the people to control nature through incessant inquiry, discovery, and innovation. Corresponding to this form of modernism is the individual's abiding faith in the capitalistic process, the quest for ultimate achievement, competition, and success and an assumption that the values that stem from such a view of life represent a truthful existence. Within this form of modernism, reason, rationality, and truth are equated with the free and creative individual. In short, this typifies a fiercely competitive free market just like the educational quest for grades and higher IQ scores. This illustrates the social efficiency movement previously alluded to. In the modern sense, school naturally leads students to competitive and unequal relations of production in what I and others would agree is the false guise of a quality institution. Thus, although tracking may seem necessary in the long run for the economy, it really divides and conquers students and forces them into functional and relegated unequal spaces in the work force.

Second, another form of modernism takes on some very important critical theory (critical pedagogy) elements of social critique, much of which both Dewey and the Frankfurt school would support. Within this form of modernism, there is hope for personal and public enlightenment. There is a deep-rooted commitment to democracy and community (Habermas, 1981). Through individual reason and ongoing reflection, there evolves a unity of the individual and society in an ongoing vision of human development, emancipation, and possibility for individual and communal betterment. Liberty and justice become the emancipatory modernistic guiding principles. These utopian dreams, it must be argued, are not unworthy. It could also be argued that these dreams are for an idealized democracy, one that the former view of modernism cannot achieve fully because of its inherent contradiction (for our purposes, the schools' ability to divide students unequally, despite rhetoric of equal opportunity of education for all members of the educational community).

In part, it could be argued that schools equate very well with the first form of modernism as evidenced by ongoing achievement tests, rating scales, stereotypes, and the like, although these may speak concurrently of schools as producing forms of community, nurture, compassion, and care. Indeed, these two forms of modernism do exist in schools. Certainly, a function of schools is to produce good, upstanding, moral citizens who are part of a democratic community. However, with the emphasis on the schools' relation to the economy as more vital, schools take on more of the first part of modernism at the expense of schools as sites of democratic possibility. Clearly, John Dewey would have aligned with the second form of modernism, as did theorists from the Frankfurt school of thought, in which enlightenment must be built within experience, reflection, critique and eventual action.

POSTMODERNISM

Contrasted to modernism, postmodernism negates world views held together by absolutes. In a postmodern world view, universal truth is abandoned (Lyotard, 1984, 1993) in lieu of asking questions such as these: Whose world view is it we are trying to understand? How is identity constructed—singularly or by the group? How and whose knowledge is transmitted? How many ways do people learn? How many realities are there? Conservatively, postmodernism delves into multiple interpretations, otherwise known as phenomenology or hermeneutics.

The part of postmodernism I associate with as related to critical pedagogy could be termed *critical postmodernism*. Critical postmodernism, like other forms of modernism, shares a similar quest for human emancipation and liberation. Yet, critical postmodernism's main concern is politically aligned with unravelling social, cultural, and human difference with an eye to a shift of consciousness into challenging and transforming both unequal relations of power and undoing forms of oppression, alienation, and subordination. Regarding teachers, this may include the struggle to overcome oppressive teacher conditions such as dehumanizing rating scales, accountability schemes, standardized curricula, and authoritarian administrators and their guiding bureaucracies.

In addition, critical postmodernism is about real people struggling in the everyday world within their multishaped identities and subjectivities. Simply put, what the relations of race, class, and gender may be to any individual will always be different and changing and forever in flux. For example, today I am not only a husband, father, ex-husband, son, lover, colleague, writer, professor, actor, sportsman, or friend. I am all these in shifting moments, mixed at various times during the day. As a student and teacher, my past history in institutions taught me that there were many hats I had to wear for survival. Central to a critical postmodern stance is the value of human differences—with the intent to undermine those forces of control that make democracy difficult to attain, like a market logic thought process that relegates schools, teachers, students, and parents into sterile creatures losing site of the ethical in lieu of both personal gain and political agendas.

Critical pedagogy, then, has its deep seated roots in the Frankfurt school's response to social inequities and Dewey's call for the inherent need to base school curricula on children's experiences. *Critical pedagogists* commonly share a conviction that if experience is rooted in reflection and our ultimate goal is human emancipation from forms of oppression, alienation, and subordination, then to be a critical pedagogist is to seriously take on this daunting challenge in the face of a social system that has historically been constructed, at least in educational terms, around a social efficiency ideology. Of course, there are multitudinous and better constructed definitions of critical pedagogy (Ellsworth, 1989; Freire & Macedo, 1995; Giroux, 1992, 1994; Lather, 1991; McLaren, 1994; McLaren & Hammer, 1989; Purpel & Shapiro, 1995; Simon, 1988, 1992; Slattery, 1995; among many others), but for the purposes of this chapter and this particular book, the criteria I put forth, defining critical pedagogy as a movement to subvert and change areas of school life that are alienating and oppressive, remain a democratic criterion and a moral and ethical imperative bar none. In the face of growing poverty, increasing disease, rampant violence, and mean-spiritedness[3] there is in my mind a despair around our political, social, and cultural

---

[3]This mean-spiritedness can be seen in the alarming poverty rates (Lipsitz, 1994), gaps between wealthy and poor (Associated Press, 1995), federally cut food and nutrition programs (Reynolds, 1995), and Black poverty and hunger (Sklar, 1993), among other startling social and economic facts that, if taken seriously, must probe the questions: Are we really a democracy? Does freedom mean starvation?

climate that makes critical pedagogy a viable and joyful response and eventual alternative to mainstream school conditions.

Critical pedagogy's response, for the most part, grounded in personal oppressive experience and hope to change those experiences, is centered around what critical pedagogist's call "voice" (McLaren, 1994), those multifaceted experiences that describe each owner's history and subjectivity.[4] Perhaps a pioneer in this realm was Paulo Freire, who until today remains an icon in critical circles, the "John Dewey" of the present era. Freire's basic assumptions were that oppressed peoples could challenge their life form by understanding the structural constraints that originally set them up as unequal members of society. More than Dewey, Freire's pedagogy was overtly political, summoning peasants to rise against social injustices. It was not just experiences that they were interrogating or that Freire advocates in reflecting on. It is language and ideas that must also be challenged, a language that guides our actions, behavior, and thoughts. Freire's (1970, 1973) method, which worked well for the underclass, can be adopted on any personal level, if the aim is to understand how social experience is constructed and ultimately how we as social actors are part of oppressive social structures. Presently, one way that critical pedagogists help define struggle is through the understanding of narrative.

THE NARRATIVE AS TEXT

Within Freire's work lies the possibility of a macro- and micro-understanding of social structures. By hearing the everyday occurrences of individuals (their struggles, etc.) and by understanding their daily experiences, be they oppressive or not, each individual was or is represented by a micro-narrative—their particular life story. To be socially and culturally transformative, this micro-narrative must be understood within the context of a larger macro-narrative—those rules and regulations that conform to science and various theories.

In this text, for instance, the macro-narrative is a critical theory discourse. This discourse assumes certain functions. First, it is highly theoretical. Second, theory must be applied to practice, whose ultimate aim is to free individuals from domination. And, within this form of narrative, there exists all forms of micro-

---

[4]The concept of "voice" is dealt with throughout this book in greater detail in various chapters.

narratives—those "voices" of the everyday person whose struggles represent and illuminate the macro-narrative. For instance Freire's work with peasants was a micro-narrative in action within a macro-narrative "critical theory/critical pedagogy" discourse!

As a form of postmodern methodology, critical social theorists in education, especially feminist theorists such as Kathleen Weiler (1987) and Madeline Grumet (1988), as well as a host of others, have used narrative as a means to capture the conditions of marginalized females, be they teachers or administrators. Narrative allows the subject to be his or her own authority. Subjects' life stories and meaning structures link human phenomena into comprehensible endeavors (Polkinghorne, 1988). These above micro-narrative accounts are well supported in the education field, within a macro-"critical" discourse, such as by Ellsworth (1989), Lather (1991), Gordon, (1995), Noddings (1992), Stone (1994), and many more feminist theorists. Additionally, various "critical" macro-theorists in multiculturalism such as Darder (1991), Sleeter and Grant (1994), Kanpol and McLaren (1995), and a host of authors, too many to name here, are supported by micro-accounts such as Pierce (1995), Yeo (1995), SooHoo (1995), and Kanpol (1995a).

This book, too, should be seen as a narrative. Different areas of critical theory are discussed in an introductory fashion. The reader should keep in mind that this macro-narrative originates from a critical tradition, historically constructed as a response to the social and cultural "savage inequalities" of our times. There will be times, within this macro-account, that I diverge to stories (micro-accounts) that can be used as a bridge with the critical tradition (macro-discourse) that this book emanates from. With that in mind I now turn to an outline of the chapters that follow.

This book is divided into three sections. The first section, of which this is the first chapter, views the *Development of Critical Pedagogy,* by coming to terms with its basic tenets. Chapter 2 argues that in order to establish a critical pedagogical framework, personal narratives (micro) related to one's own history, faith, subordination, oppression, as well as acts of compliance to the dominant structures must be understood in order to feed into a "critical" mindset. Thus, stories from my own past as related to schools, religion, and fundamental values are described and set within the theoretical understanding of the previous chapter.

Chapter 3 outlines the various ways in which a central critical pedagogy tenet—resistance theory—can be viewed. Institutional and cultural political resistance is analyzed with special considerations as to how this may relate both personally (intellectually and practically) and institutionally. Relatedly, resistance theory is viewed through some analysis of former case studies (micro-narrative accounts) and is related back to chapter 2 accounts.

Part II is entitled *Ongoing Critical Pedagogy Trends*. Chapter 4 illustrates critical pedagogy's response to the multicultural (diversity) effort and strategies currently being utilized within education. It is argued that multiculturalism can be viewed from many perspectives (conservative, liberal, and critical). From the "critical" perspective, multiculturalism must be viewed as an alternative to traditional views that have historically tended to work against true democratic intents.

Chapter 5 views how teachers have been historically portrayed through gender, specifically female; how teachers have been stereotyped to act, behave, and think in certain ways, all under "male"-dominated influence. Among other things, this chapter analyzes how schools have systematically defined the dominating educational discourse (empowerment, professionalism, effective teaching, etc.) along partial gender lines. As a conclusion to this chapter, a closer look at how feminists have contributed so importantly to critical pedagogy is discussed.

Chapter 6 is co-authored with a former urban teacher and elementary school principal. We argue that for schools to become critical sites of possibility, principals in particular will have to be educated and empowered in critical ways, particularly through viewing key educational terms in multiple forms (empowerment, literacy, etc.). This chapter outlines strategies and methods that have these critical elements to them and that can be used by principals as a guide to start viewing schools as "critical" sites of social change.

Chapter 7's contribution is by Professor Fred Yeo, a former urban educator and now a professor of educational foundations. After my introduction to the chapter, which discusses the need for critical pedagogy to "invest" in urban education, Professor Yeo narrates and analyzes his personal experiences in the ghettos of Los Angeles, particularly in light of some of critical pedagogy's major tenets.

Part III is titled *Emerging Critical Pedagogy Trends*. I view this section as encompassing new and revitalized ideas in critical pedagogy. It should be noted that this section is merely the tip of the iceberg regarding critical pedagogy's newest trends. Areas such as Gay Studies in Education or Chicano resistance movements, for instance, are among some of these emerging trends not necessarily discussed. Nevertheless, some new trends are elaborated on. Chapter 8 argues that a new teaching paradigm can or must be viewed as an alternative to the present status quo-type methods. Popular culture has gained a significant space in critical pedagogical circles, which previously were viewed as outside of the educational arena. Henry Giroux has been a pioneer in his efforts to bring these ideas to the educational arena. It is argued that popular culture deserves space and must be incorporated as a pedagogical element in all phases of teacher education programs, especially if the programs are to be true to their democratic ideals. Through analyzing a text by Henry Giroux on popular culture, I further argue that qualitative research and "text" can be viewed through the medium of media as a way to reach the "affective investments" of students so as to challenge their perspectives on teaching and the technocratic role of teachers in the social order.

Chapter 9 argues that school reform, particularly Outcomes Based Education, can and should become both more critical and more normative within its frameworks in order for democracy to thrive. A normative case is made to incorporate critical pedagogy as part of policy procedures.

Finally, the concluding Chapter 10 argues that critical pedagogy has now come to the stage in which a new and revitalized language must be sought as a "language of possibility." Reflecting back on my own micro-accounts, this chapter argues that critical pedagogy must transcend the issues mentioned in this book and be connected spiritually to its cause for hope to change the present conditions.

At the conclusion of each chapter I present the instructor who uses this book with what I perceive to be possible classroom activities related to the chapter topics. Following this, there is a question for discussion section. I hope that this part of the chapter is used by the instructor as a guide rather than etched in stone.

As I head into the next chapter I remind readers of the intent of this book. What follows is not high-brow theory. I hope to make critical theory, particularly as it relates to education, understandable in light of the everyday micro-accounts we all live in. I also hope that these chapters introduce readers to and are fairly representative of some of the *Issues and Trends in Critical Pedagogy*, and that the struggle for a critical pedagogy, historically constructed, will continue not in vain, but with joyous commitment and love for our fellow person.

CLASSROOM ACTIVITIES

1. a. Have some students "research" social efficiency and others research John Dewey.
   b. Set up a debate between the two groups allowing for both philosophies to be further elaborated on.
2. Let students share both through group work and writing activities on how their schools were either part of the social efficiency or progressive educational system.
3. Within group work again and/or classroom debate, set up both a modern and postmodern scenario. What would "modern" as well as "postmodern" education look like? Relate this to curriculum matters to enhance this response.

QUESTIONS FOR DISCUSSION

1. Describe the school as "factory" metaphor? Relate it to your own experiences.
2. What distinguishes Dewey from traditional models of education?
3. Have you ever faced oppressive and alienating experiences in and out of school? *Name* them and discuss how one might avoid having those experiences again or changing the nature of them.
4. What is your narrative? How many identities do you have?

REFERENCES

Anyon, J. (1980). Social class and the hidden curriculum of work. *Journal of Education, 162*(2), 67-92.

Anyon, J. (1979). Ideology and U.S. history textbooks. *Harvard Educational Review, 49*(3), 381-386.

Apple, M. (1982). *Education and power.* Boston: Routledge & Kegan Paul.

Apple, M. (1983). *Teachers and texts.* New York: Routledge.

Associated Press. (1995, October 28). Global study: US has widest gap between rich and poor. *Chicago Tribune*, Section 1, p. 21.

Bowles, S., & Gintis, H. (1976). *Schooling in capitalist America*. New York: Basic Books.

Capper, C., & Jamison, M. (1993). Outcome based education reexamined: From structural functionalism to poststructuralism. *Educational Policy, 7*(4), 427-446.

Darder, A. (1991). *Culture and power in the classroom*. Westport, CT: Bergin & Garvey.

Dewey, J. (1902a). *The child and the curriculum*. Chicago: The University of Chicago Press.

Dewey, J. (1902b). *The school and society*. Chicago: The University of Chicago Press.

Dewey, J. (1909). *Moral principles in education*. Boston: Houghton Mifflin.

Dewey J. (1916). *Democracy and education*. New York: Free Press.

Dewey, J. (1929). *Individualism: Old and new*. New York: Capricorn Books.

Dewey, J. (1938). *Education and experience*. New York: Collier Macmillan Canada Inc.

Dewey, J. (1939). *Freedom and culture*. New York: G.P. Putnam's Sons.

Ellsworth, E. (1989). Why doesn't this feel empowering? Working through the repressive myths of critical pedagogy. *Harvard Educational Review, 59*(3), 297-324.

Freire, P. (1970). *Pedagogy of the oppressed*. New York: Continuum.

Freire, P. (1973). *Education for critical consciousness*. New York: Seabury Press.

Freire P., & Macedo, D. (1995).A Dialogue: Culture, language, and race. *Harvard Educational Review, 65*(3), 377-402.

Gaines, D (1992). *Teenage wasteland*. New York: HarperCollins.

Giroux, H. (1983). *Theory and resistance in education*. Westport, CT: Bergin & Garvey.

Giroux, H. (1992). *Border crossings*. New York: Routledge.

Giroux, H. (1994). *Disturbing pleasures*. New York: Routledge.

Gordon, B. (1995). The fringe dwellers: African American women scholars in the postmodern era. In B. Kanpol & P. McLaren (Eds.), *Critical multiculturalism. Uncommon voices in a common struggle* (pp. 59-88). Westport, CT: Bergin & Garvey.

Grumet, M. (1988). *Bitter milk: Women and teaching*. Amherst: University of Massachusetts Press.

Habermas, J. (1981). *The theory of communicative action: Reason and rationality in society*. Boston: Beacon Press.

hooks, b. (1989). *Talking back: Thinking feminism, thinking Black*. Boston: South End Press.

hooks, b. (1994). *Teaching to transgress*. New York: Routledge.

Kanpol, B. (1994). *Critical pedagogy: An introduction.* Westport, CT: Bergin & Garvey.

Kanpol, B. (1995a). Multiculturalism and empathy: A border pedagogy of solidarity. In B. Kanpol & P. McLaren (Eds.). *Critical multiculturalism* (pp. 177-196). Westport, CT: Bergin & Garvey.

Kanpol, B. (1995b). Outcome-bases education and democratic commitment: Hopes and possibilities. *Educational Policy, 9*(4), 359-374.

Kanpol, B., & McLaren, P. (Eds.). (1995). *Critical multiculturalism: Uncommon voices in a common struggle.* Westport, CT: Bergin & Garvey.

Kozol, J. (1991). *Savage inequalities.* New York: Crown.

Kozol, J. (1994). *Grace under fire.* New York: Crown.

Lather, P. (1991). *Getting smart. Feminist research and pedagogy with/in the postmodern.* London: Routledge.

Lipsitz, G. (1994). We know what time it is: Race, class and youth culture in the nineties. In A. Ross & T. Ross (Eds.), *Microphone friends* (pp. 52-53). New York: Routledge.

Lyotard, J. (1984). *The postmodern condition: A report on knowledge.* Minneapolis: University of Minnesota Press.

Lyotard, J. (1993). *The postmodern explained* (J. Pefanis & M. Thomas, Trans. & Eds.). Minneapolis: University of Minnesota Press.

McCall, N. (1994). *Makes me want to holler.* New York: Vintage.

McLaren, P. (1994). *Life in schools.* New York: Longman.

McLaren, P., & Hammer, R. (1989). Critical pedagogy and the postmodern challenge. *Educational Foundations, 3*(3), 29-62.

McQuaide, J., & Pliska, M. (1993). The challenge to Pennsylvania's education reform. *Educational Leadership, 51*(4), 16-18.

National Commission on Excellence in Education. (1983). Washington, DC: U.S. Government Printing Office.

Nieto, S. (1996). *Affirming diversity* (2nd ed.).New York: Longman.

Noddings, N. (1992). *The challenge to care in schools.* New York: Teachers College Press.

Oakes, J. (1985). *Keeping track: How schools structure inequality.* New Haven, CT: Yale University Press.

Pierce, B. (1995). Learning the hard way: Maria's story. In B. Kanpol & P. McLaren (Eds.), *Critical multiculturalism* (pp. 167-176). Westport, CT: Bergin & Carvey.

Polkinghorne, D. (1988). *Narrative knowing and the human sciences.* Albany: State University of New York Press.

Purpel, D., & Shapiro, S. (1995). *Beyond liberation and excellence.* Westport, CT: Bergin & Garvey.

Reynolds, B. (1995, November 17). Now we've learned who Clinton is not. *USA Today* p. 15A.

Shapiro, S. (1985). Capitalism at risk: The political economy of educational reports of 1983. *Educational Theory, 35*(1).

Shapiro, S. (1990). *Between capitalism and democracy.* Westport, CT: Bergin & Garvey.

Simon, R. (1988). For a pedagogy of possibility. *Critical Pedagogy Networker, 1*(1), 1-5.

Simon, R. (1992). *Teaching against the grain.* Westport, CT: Bergin & Garvey.

Slattery, P. (1995). *Curriculum development in the postmodern era.* New York: Garland.

Sleeter, C., & Grant, C. (1994). *Making choices for multicultural education.* New York: Macmillan.

SooHoo, S. (1995). Emerging student and teacher voices: A syncopated rhythm in public education. In B. Kanpol & P. McLaren. (Eds.), *Critical multiculturalism* (pp. 217-234). Westport, CT: Bergin & Garvey.

Spring, J. (1989). *The sorting machine revisited. National educational policy since 1945.* New York: Longman

Spring, J. (1993). *The American school.* New York: McGraw-Hill.

Spring, J. (1994). *Wheels in the head. Educational philosophies of authority and culture from Socrates to Paulo Freire.* New York: McGraw-Hill.

Stone, L. (1994). *A feminist reader in education.* New York: Routledge & Kegan Paul.

Weiler, K. (1987). *Women teaching for change.* Westport, CT: Bergin & Garvey.

West, C. (1982). *Prophesy deliverance: An African-American revolutionary Christianity.* Philadelphia: The Westminster Press.

West, C. (1993). *Prophetic reflections.* Monroe, ME: Common Courage Press.

Yeo, F. (1995). The conflicts of difference in an inner-city school: Experiencing border crossings in the ghetto. In B. Kanpol & P. McLaren (Eds.), *Critical multiculturalism* (pp. 197-216). Westport, CT: Bergin & Garvey.

2

A PERSONAL JOURNEY: ESTABLISHING A CRITICALITY

Probably a defining moment for any critical theorist is their personal understanding of the oppressive structures they formerly or presently live in. As a critical theorist (critical pedagogist), I too have a micro-narrative, or life stories, replete with instances in which I could see and feel forms of personal alienation, oppression, and subordination that I was subject to as well as an instigator of. All these instances, in some part, form a cornerstone of my politics, a part of my construction of a "critical" pedagogical position, a political response to the conditions of everyday experiences, to the values that embody me and the culture I live in. With that in mind, this chapter focuses on parts of my own narrative. I do this in part to vulnerably share some of my history so that you the reader can perhaps begin to think of your personal history in a "critical" light.

I was born to two very proper folks, in Melbourne, Australia. My father was/is an extremely hard-working man. My mother was/is a devoted wife. She was always around when I needed her, invested in my daily activities that included school work and outside interests such as my sporting concerns. She was raised within an Orthodox Jewish tradition, whereas my father grew up as a Zionist (dreaming to return to Israel), still respecting and holding onto Jewish traditions. My mother's Jewish lineage consisted of a conservative religious sort. I often recall at her mother's house, the rigid Saturday rituals—no lights or television on Saturday, the Jewish Sabbath, and so on. As I grew up, the division of labor in my parent's home was very clearly divided by gender roles. My parents seemed content with that lifestyle. It was predictable and I felt safe in both their particular personal and social setup.

Both Mom and Dad had found their ways to Australia differently. In short, Dad had come through China (by way of Russian parents) and Mom through Poland. For various reasons they both were in Israel when they met: Dad through the Israeli independence war and Mom on a personal visit. They immigrated to Australia and lived there for 20 years. As Zionists they returned to Israel in 1973, with their two children, and still live there today.

Growing up in Australia was easy and safe. Although my parents struggled financially, particularly early in their marriage, through self-discipline, motivation, simple desire, and perhaps a little luck, my father became an entrepreneur and moved socially into the middle class. I never felt materialistically in need, and usually, if my parents struggled both financially and/or personally, I never knew about it. I grew up with that privilege, recalling only fleeting times when Dad would be upset when business was not going well, as is the case today.

SCHOOL EXPERIENCES

Perhaps my childhood should be divided into at least two significant areas: school and religion. I vividly recall attending a private Jewish day school. Two pronounced things happened to me during that time. School was both a bore and very competitive. Perhaps the way I described social efficiency in the previous chapter best depicts this particular school. Tracking into subject areas (usually male and female divided between humanities and sciences; males into sciences and females into humanities) was predominant. Teaching methodologies were hardly progressive: Bits of information had to be continuously memorized and regurgitated back on an upcoming test or quiz, usually given daily in some fashion. For instance, I recall well how in grades 3, 4, and 5 the same Hebrew teacher expected us to learn lists of words by heart for the following days. I understood that if I succeeded I would receive a school stamp; six stamps meant a special chocolate bar, the flavor of which still lingers in my mind when I think of the texture of those chocolates. Often, friendships were defined by the amount of chocolates we acquired and/or school stamps we had!

Fear was instilled into those who did not compete well academically (like me), as I am sure to those who did compete well and were rewarded. Students were very competitive as were parents, who often would base worth on achievement, such as Moms talking on the phone and comparing their children's grades (such as was in my case). Stereotypes were abundant and I was as guilty of conforming to and reproducing them as anyone in the school. I recall, not with honor, "fat and gross Helen," "nerd Henry," "overweight Alan," the "geniuses," and of course the "jocks and idiots," of which I was supposedly one! I am also implicated in these stereotypical structures in ways that were oppressive to both others and myself. I am not proud of this fact. I only know it is a fact, and I am sure in some fundamental way continues in some fashion whether conscious or unconsciously even today.

Teachers in this school were authoritarian as I have described in detail elsewhere (Kanpol, 1994). They were also sexist. I was usually afraid of them. At best, I recall some teachers taking an interest in me, usually pointing out to me what a good sportsman I was. That was it folks! My principal had it in for me. When I misbehaved, or stepped a little out of line, like moving to a seat next to me on the school bus, which was not allowed, the principal would comment, pushing me with his hand on my chest against a wall in his enclosed office: "Kanpol, pick your socks up son, or I'll skin you alive and hang your pieces on the wall." I was accused by the principal of smoking drugs, hanging out with the wrong people, and being a womanizer, all the while ironically a virgin and totally committed to sporting successes, so antithetical to all he was accusing me of. I was so afraid of this social efficiency system that I believe I was even forced into lying about grades (changing grades on my report card, etc.) and when tests were. I was a cheating expert, living on the edge when it came to exam time, even though I felt I had studied hard. I just was not a regimented learner. There was no freedom of expression. Perhaps this is why I did my best to fall asleep in class, listen to music through ear plugs when the teacher talked, build hypothetical football teams, and so on. Besides, I thought to myself, didn't teachers understand that some kids just learned differently?

School was a far cry from the progressive kind that Dewey both wrote and dreamed about. Curriculum was clearly not connected to personal life experiences. Democracy was thwarted by authoritarianism and patriarchal control. There was no substantive vision for why we were to receive an education, only that it would land us a more prestigious job one day, thus providing upward social mobility. The price for upward mobility, it seems now, was selling one's soul, bowing to authority without thinking, walking blindly into a tunnel, leaving the blindfold on forever, never asking questions, and receiving knowledge as if it were written in stone. And, if one was to question the knowledge, it was met with great disagreement by teachers, usually ending up in some disciplinary action, such as writing 100 times "I must not disturb the class," and so on.

As a result of this boredom, the guys in our geography class in the ninth grade came up with an innovative idea. Our teacher, a paunchy sort, always talked with a collection of ooh's and aah's, hands in his pockets or behind his back. As a reflection of this teacher (let alone subject matter, which was taught in similar mechanical ways), the guys in the class developed a mini world cricket series (baseball originated from cricket). Every ooh and aah had meaning, either a run or hit scored. Every hand behind the back or in the pocket had significant ramification for whichever team was named (either an out or the equivalent of a home run). Over the course of a year we completed our wonderful sporting event, our world series! Yes, geography was fun to go to. So irrelevant was the material that a lot of us worse students (or should I say students with low GPAs) even had fun making our Hebrew teacher cry during some classes, either by pretending to fall asleep, excessive talking, goading, and the like. Thus, at times the curriculum, so far removed from personal reality, led me and others to acts that, when I think about them, were unjust and demeaning.

As I write this, I am not proud to be part of those eventual dropouts who for want of a better life in school made some teachers pay for the school's deficiencies. I bring this to light as an example of what can happen within a system that is so stultified, that students' ways of surviving borders on the immoral. The eventual outcome of all this was my failure and dropping out of school in the 11th grade, despite my effort to study, pass, and please my parents. It seemed as if I was doomed anyway. In the eighth grade the principal of the school mentioned to my parents that "he should be a barber," "he would never pass," "he should just learn a trade," and so on. Yes, eventually I did drop out (11th grade), but, perhaps through some miracle, ended up in Israel, in an American International school and received not only my diploma, but a basketball scholarship to attend Tel Aviv University. At 20 years of age, I decided that I wanted to read, that basketball was always there for me, but I had something to prove—that I was not as dumb as I was stereotyped to be. With a lot of struggle and intense determination I completed my B.A. in the subjects I had failed in high school (English Literature and History). I was on my way!

While in Israel, one survival mechanism for me was to resort to using English as a means to earn a living. Initially that is why I became a teacher and went through a certification program in Israel.

My certification program was very much like the school I attended in Australia. Basically, we were told how to teach, prepare lesson and unit plans, dress, behave, and the like. This did not prepare me for the real world of 30 or more kids staring at me, demanding blood—mine! No mention was made of alternative teaching approaches, or discipline techniques, or social and cultural issues. By the very negation of this, I was still stuck in a socially efficient mindset, with little connection made by my professors to the lived experiences of what it may be like to connect curriculum to a 15-year-old pregnant girl, kids who smoke drugs or belong to gangs, or kids who come from broken homes with one or no parents to speak of. Teacher education prepared me for a form of modernism, in which rationality was quickly used as a sponge activity, in which social and cultural differences were smothered in lieu of nationalism, and so on.

As a teacher, I am admittedly guilty of conforming to a social efficiency system. In my certification program, no mention was made of Dewey and the progressives. So I had no option but to feel absolutely guilty about conforming to a visionless curriculum, robotic teaching methods, and the like. Do not misunderstand me here; I was still innovative at times. However, I was unprepared both in method and vision to challenge a system that was so entrenched in a market logic that I became a part of that logic whether I wanted to or not. The teachers I worked with were also embedded in this logic, so much so that curriculum meetings became gripe sessions instead of reflective times, clarification sessions on whether the curriculum was technically okay rather than a reflection on curriculum substance.

I struggle within my own teaching space in the academe as well. And, even though I found my way to the United States in 1983, and completed my Ph.D. in social foundations, many of the same problems I encountered in my past presently exist. I now teach foundations courses in a system that concurrently failed but also made me. Yet I talk about my own deficiencies, limitations, and the like, all the while getting students to challenge their own personal limitations and relationships to forms of alienation, oppression, and subordination. Students reflect on the weaknesses of their certification program—the social efficiency mindsets they face daily both in and out of the academe. Teaching for me presents a platform to both critique the present social and cultural structure as well as find ways to etch out possibility and hope in the face of social efficiency nightmares. Perhaps a part of this challenge is personally related to issues of values embedded within faith.

There is another part to my narrative that has not been mentioned thus far. Even though I grew up in a traditionally kept Jewish home (which Mum always tried to ritualistically keep through Friday night candle lighting, Kosher food, and more), little mention or personal analysis and scrutiny was made of this impact on my life in my early years, particularly as it relates to everyday experiences. I only know that I challenged going to synagogue, and so on.

Much like some religious schools (McLaren, 1993), religion was (as I felt at the time) forced on me through prayer and ritual. I recall having to recite certain prayers every morning as well as attend Hebrew classes twice daily. I distinctly remember my Hebrew teacher of three grades. Endless vocabulary learning, meaningless rote exercises, and Hebrew became a sick joke! As mentioned previously, I along with others was not going to be forced to learn an alien language, even if it was, as my parents explained "in my best interests." Yes, I was, along with others, resentful of anything that was authoritatively forced and denying me freedom of thoughtful expression.

Despite my personal struggles in this Jewish school, being "forced" to learn for Barmitzvah rituals was still rather enjoyable. I wanted to make my parents proud and, additionally, I would be able to showcase my talents, which I did. My Barmitzvah to this day remains etched as a major memory in my life in a number of ways. I fondly recall the weekend celebration as the center of attention with family and friends gathering from all over the country. I guess entrance into Jewish "manhood" was a big deal. So I played on, although I was never told why this was important, only that it was. I was the good kid and acquiesced to what was required of me, even though I disliked the methods of forced Hebrew instruction in my school. Despite the centrality of my Barmitzvah to Jewish experiences of the community, I was bogged down personally with academic requirements to the point that I had to lie before my Barmitzvah as to the grade I received for a test or even about a test I took two days earlier. Despite the glory and symbolic significance of this Jewish ritual, I wondered even then if a part of this ritual included fear of performance and testing and living up to expectations. Who was I chanting in synagogue for? I did not understand what I was singing (reminds me of school experiences— not knowing why I was learning certain bits of information), even though the Rabbi made a point of telling the congregation that he felt that "Barry sang as if he knew what every word meant." When he said that I knew I had good acting qualities in me.

It was after my Barmitzvah that I suddenly shot up in height and, as it was also a time of adolescence, I began to seriously think about my role as a member of society—both in and out of school. Personal identity was questioned, particularly with my family's impending immigration to Israel. I started to interrogate (less then than today, of course) those "dangerous memories" that Sharon Welch (1990) talks about, those memories of alienation and personal oppression that guide action for personal and possible social change.

Thus going to synagogue grew to be a forced commitment I began to resent, particularly after my entrance into "Jewish manhood." While I was growing up, synagogue was not a place of prayer or worship so much as it seemed like a place of social mobility and/or a social outlet, even though I fondly recall attending synagogue as a 6-year-old with my grandfather. As a kid I loved this. I appreciated his personal attention and the games we played during services, most of which I have replicated with my daughters. In the long run, however, I attended synagogue rarely, mainly on the high holidays. And it was a chore. It seemed weird to be told to pray twice or three times a year for forgiveness of one's sins, particularly on Yom Kippur (Day of Atonement). Why should I atone when I felt I was being shafted by a system in which I was defined by my principal as a failure of life, a nonsuccess, a womanizer, smoker of drugs, and so on? So although I may have personally "sinned" (not even knowing what these sins were even as I didn't know why I was atoning), so did the social efficiency institution I was living in. What about the other 362 days of the year I would think to myself. Besides, when I attended synagogue at the time, I could not understand the Hebrew and the hymns sung. Little sense was thus made over mandatory services. Why was I challenging these traditions—or, put more bluntly, forced attendance at another (what I perceived to be) social efficiency model? These questions could not be answered then, but as part of my "dangerous memories" must always be interrogated for further explanation, understanding, interpretation, and reconfiguring. This is part of a reflection on experiences, a necessary condition for a "critical pedagogical" mindset.

I really do not want to remain cynical, for not all is or was that negative. I warmly recall reading Old Testament Bible stories late into the night in my bed before I would doze off. I would read these stories over and again—stories of creation, Adam and Eve (and their story of deceit, questioning authority, etc.), Cain and Abel (and the story of greed and competitiveness), Noah (and his story of faith), Abraham (and his story of both faith and commitment), Jacob, Moses (and his story of challenging the Egyptian oppressors and leading the Hebrews out of slavery), Pharoah (and his dictatorship), David (and his sexism, struggles as an underdog, etc.), Jonathan, Samson and Ruth, and so on. I learned what miracles in the desert were, a covenant, yes, God's promises, and more. I believed it all! I was fascinated. Would I ever have a personal covenant? Could I be special like those Biblical heroes? They were larger than life figures!

Today, I often reflect on how those stories brought and to some degree still bring me safety and joy, especially today and in my troubled child spirit then. I even remember, as I write now, the smell of the pages those stories were written on. They were etched in my memory forever, even though the encyclopedia I read them out of seems ancient today. Often, when visiting my parents in Israel, I return to those stories and muse through them recalling very fond memories.

I joyfully recall Passover and the Jewish New Year and the various rituals celebrated with my family. Even though I was not taught so much of what the profound symbolic ramifications of these rituals were, they were nonetheless the stuff that held families together, and I appreciated them then as I do now. What really fascinated me were stories of escape, justice, freedom, martyrdom, and commitment to a "promised land," and so on. Perhaps that is why my parents are in Israel today. And perhaps that is why I am in the field I am in today—justice, freedom, escape, and the like.

DISCRIMINATION

Very sadly I was met with a fair amount of antisemitism as a child growing up. "Dirty Jew" and Jew boy" were often flung at me in discriminating and humiliating ways. Playing competitive sports for non-Jewish teams was never easy because I often felt left out, different, and at times "less than." I would try to hide my identity. And, although I did not go out of my way to tell my non-Jewish friends "who" I was, everyone knew I was Jewish. Relatedly, but just as important, I grew up in a closed Jewish community who *also* discriminated against non-Jews. I would often hear the words "Those Goyim" (non-Jews) as a statement of Jewish retaliation to "Those Jews" or "Dirty Jew." And, in the street where I lived from 8 to 17 years of age, many kids were not allowed to play with us because we were Jewish. Until today I *despise* both forms of Jewish and non-Jewish discrimination! Most sadly, I grew up with both guilt and shame at being Jewish—an interesting dualism because I was always taught to be proud of my heritage. I would often walk to synagogue on the Day of Atonement and have to pass a public school (it was called Brighton High). I would see kids staring at me—at my suit and tie. Or was I just paranoid? I quickly learned to walk across the street from the school so as to avoid more shame. My hiding had deeper ramifications, all of which is still difficult to make sense of today.

As I grew up through my formative years I learned that truth was supposedly a Jewish thing. There was no mention of meaning making beyond the Old Testament. I grew up not even knowing about the possibility of either a New Testament or what the difference historically was between Jew, Gentile, or Christian, or about the appreciation of differences in general. Joy, love, and comfort was again supposedly a Jewish thing, which, according to my personal experiences, were remote given the realities of forced religion, the authoritarian structure of the Jewish school I attended, the discrimination of both Jews and non-Jews, and the feelings of guilt and shame I had. Who needed this stuff I would always inwardly retort.

Since those days, life's experiences have had a way of humbling me. As a struggling immigrant to Israel I often met the discriminating forces of people. "You'll never speak the correct Hebrew" I was often told by the dominant culture, leaving me with a feeling of subordination and "less" than in general. I would not really become Israeli if I did not enter the army (which I did not believe in). I was basically illiterate in the language—I had a third-grade reading level at best after years of living there and I could not follow the news at 100%—even 80%. Besides, I always had a foreign accent and had to repeat my self over and again. My biggest danger was feeling superior to the general Israeli because I was Anglo. Maybe, in fact, it was me who was stereotyping that culture as less than. Maybe it was me who was not being culturally sensitive. Dangerous memories will help me realize how I was both oppressed and concurrently oppressed others. Dangerous memories will remind me of a failed marriage: patriarchal domination, lack of sensitivity, issues of control, and power on both sides. Dangerous memories will remind me of a career that sits entrenched in theoretical nihilism and despair, which have often rendered me quite sarcastic, hopeless, and sorry in the face of social, cultural, and structural nightmares—this despite my privileged social position!

My politics has often been confusing. No wonder. Despite the postmodern insistence on multiple realities and never-ending deconstruction, I have often wondered what meaning I can take from my youth and present life that makes storytelling so powerful, so profound, and so real that a politics of hope can rear its head. So I feel that I must take those biblical stories of joy and seek every emancipatory moment out of them. I must challenge traditional Jewish ways, or even social efficient systems, as I did as a boy, and read for myself the New Testament or/and create possibility out of a simple and mechanistic mindset. It becomes my duty as a critical pedagogist to etch out progressive possibilities, as people like Martin Luther King did, and others beforehand and subsequently to literally see those "dangerous memories" in the face of despair, with the intent to find joy and hope for a better way than "savage inequalities" depicts.

CONCLUSION

In presenting this book I realize that critical pedagogy is not only about one tradition or one faith. For instance, I humbly admit that I have learned from the Black Church movement, particularly from people such as Cornel West (1993), bell hooks (1989), James Cone (1970), and Manning Marable (1992). I have also learned from Dorothee Soelle (1984) and Sharon Welch (1990). They have all taught me that "faith," however one defines it, can be a good thing. They have, for instance, within a critical tradition, sought justice, connected feminism to spirituality, a form of what Noddings (1992) may mean by "care." In the face of doubt and uncertainty, within a structural socially efficient managed system, scholars such as David Purpel (1989), Abraham Heschel (1965) and Michael Lerner (1994) have taught me that even Judaism can and must be more than middle-class talk and, like any faith or belief, transcend our own mortal and finite being. Critical pedagogy must take our imaginations and guide us beyond the possible into the probable, through experience, reflection, and critique to joy and possibility as acts of solidarity and witness to one another.

Heading into the following chapters, readers should reflectively remind themselves how their life story (their history) has impacted their social world. Although the next chapters depict trends in critical pedagogy, readers of this text would do well to always reflect on their relationship to the issues—resistance theory, multiculturalism or popular culture, and so on. Let your history intrude on the content and messages of critical pedagogy.

CLASSROOM ACTIVITIES

1. a. Have students build a family tree.
   b. As an assignment find out all one can about their family, searching for patterns of behavior and thoughts in which the student is implicated.
2. Within groups, let students share their findings.
3. Have students both discuss and write about "dangerous memories" from their perspective.

QUESTIONS FOR DISCUSSION

1. Describe any discriminatory forces that you have encountered in your life.
2. As a present or future teacher, discuss how you would go about various happenings in the school day when you do not necessarily agree with them (such as discipline procedures, state-mandated curriculum, enforcement of social divisions both in social class and gender bifurcations, etc.).
3. After reading this chapter, can you redefine your response to the last question in the last chapter which asked: What is your narrative, and how many identities do you have?

REFERENCES

Cone, J. (1970). *A Black theology of liberation.* New York: J.B. Lippincott.

Heschel, A. (1965). *Who is man?* Stanford, CA: Stanford University Press.

hooks, b. (1989) *Talking back: Thinking feminism, thinking Black.* Boston, MA: South End Press.

Kanpol, B. (1994) *Critical pedagogy: An introduction.* Westport, CT: Bergin & Garvey.

Lerner, M. (1994). *Jewish renewal: A path to healing and transformation.* New York: G.P. Putnam's Sons.

Marable, M. (1992). *The crisis of color and democracy.* Monroe ME: Common Courage Press.

McLaren, P. (1993). *Teaching as a ritual performance: Toward a political economy of educational symbols and gestures.* New York: Routledge & Kegan Paul.

Noddings, N. (1992). *The challenge to care in schools.* New York: Teachers College Press.

Purpel, D. (1989). *The moral and spiritual crisis in education.* Westport, CT: Bergin & Garvey.

Soelle, D. (1984). *To work and to love: A theology of creation.* Philadelphia: Fortress Press.

Welch, S. (1990). *A feminist ethic of risk.* Minneapolis: Fortress Press.

West, C. (1993). *Race matters.* Boston: Beacon Press.

3

CRITICAL PEDAGOGY AND THE CONCEPT OF RESISTANCE

No doubt, as a student, or preservice and eventual public school teacher, a certain frustration and/or anger seemed to boil within me. I can say now with clarity that these feelings resulted from the boredom I faced at school, the contradictions in my teacher education program, and the lack of autonomy as a teacher. I would often react to all this through various acts: falling asleep in class; challenging the teacher's authority; coming late to teacher's meetings, and the like. What I didn't understand at the time, was the symbolic significance of these acts. They had the seeds of a much deeper resistance in them. These acts can be connected to the critical education literature.

In the domain of radical education literature, it is worth noting that the 1970s, 1980s, and 1990s have highlighted the centrality of sociological interpretations of schools, particularly in the forms of ethnographies and personal micro-narratives. The impetus propelling this research has been to both describe and debate as well as critically engage with how actors/persons actually construct knowledge and meaning in their lives, particularly that knowledge and meaning that both conforms to and deviates from the dominant and at times oppressive discourses of our society. Indeed, discerning behavior from an actor's perspective (teacher, student, or anyone else

33

in school for that matter, as is the central concern of this book) and making the essential connections within the larger social structure, or macro narratives, has become a major agenda over the years for radical educational ethnographers or theorists.

More recent pioneers in this critical field began with the issues of understanding how schools acted as social control mechanisms (Young, 1971), to understanding how schools portrayed a hidden curriculum (Giroux, 1983) espousing forms of knowledge and power defined by a capitalistic market logic (Apple, 1979, 1982; Shapiro, 1990), much like the social efficiency movement of the 1920s, to studies of students taking on the system through overt actions of resistance (Willis, 1977).

The past several years have generated numerous studies of student resistance (McLaren, 1993; Willis, 1977; Yeo, 1996; to name but a few), but notably less on teacher resistance. In the main, these studies have dealt with how social processes (such as forms of control, authority relations and autonomy, etc.) are negotiated through the actions of actors (Everhart, 1983; Willis, 1977; Woods, 1986). Certainly, as has been noted, the ethnographic investigation of the experiences of both students and teachers is both problematic and complex (Apple & Weis, 1983; Bullough & Gitlin, 1985; Hargreaves, 1984; Willis, 1977). Clearly, for instance, Willis's (1977) study of a group of working-class students he named the "lads" presents a picture of creative intelligence by a group of deviant 16- to 17-year-old boys who challenged institutional authority for very good reasons: School in general connected little to their everyday experiences, as the curriculum did not. The school's middle-class competitive logic simply made no sense to the lads.

Yet, within their personal group solidarity and challenges to institutional authority (teachers, individualism, etc.), they still reproduced a working-class, sexist, and racist culture, and thus damned their own resistances into eventual failure by succumbing to tracking themselves into the working class culture they were born into. Social mobility was out. A more egalitarian society was not struggled for. Thus, as part of a social efficiency system, through their resistances, the "lads" merely reproduced their own social class. It seems to me that, notably absent in all these studies, such as Willis's, has been a clearer understanding of how the concept of "resistance" can be viewed as more of a hopeful and emancipatory sign.

MY OWN STUDIES

My own completed case studies on teachers (Kanpol, 1994) was an effort to understand the resistant cultures of teachers. Three case studies over the past few years focused on what I believed to be countercultural traits. Clearly, the method for doing these studies has been somewhat problematic. For instance, in the first study, in a middle school, a group of eighth-grade teachers notably created their own counterculture to offset what they believed to be an inept administration. Yet, in the process of their behavior, this group of teachers merely worked harder, making the principal look good downtown. This justified the teachers bending policy and creating rule-breaking activities. Apart from one or two instances, no dent so to speak was made into changing oppressive and dominating attitudes by themselves or as a group. One of the methodological problems I faced as an ethnographer was to distance my self from the teachers. Yet, given my history as a teacher and the problems I had experienced with administration's oft socially efficient mentality, gaining objectivity was not possible.

In my second study, situated in an elementary school, I followed merely one teacher (this can be considered a methodological weakness, for how valid can data be with one subject?) for a year to see how she challenged the principal's damning logic, depicting minority students and others in this particular school as possessing a "blue collar vocational future." What I found in this study was that Betty was able, in the process of teaching global education, to challenge students to think beyond their particular stereotype, to be creative, to challenge forms of individualism and what I defined as negative competition (Kanpol, 1994, chap. 4). I also learned that unless teachers are able to understand their own oppressive experiences, the curriculum they chose to teach would be less meaningful for both teacher and student. For Betty, it was imperative that not only she alter her own life, but those of her students as well—and that meant challenging forms of alienation, oppression, and subordination. Betty's official and hidden curriculum was both consciously and unconsciously used for this purpose.

My third study took place in a high school that boasted a 98% minority population. The thought of studying a school with 3,000 students was daunting, as was finding teachers to be in this study. Eventually five teachers volunteered to be involved in my research. Clearly, the methodological problem revolved around why others did not choose to be a part of my study and why these five teachers did: What vested interests did they have? What vested interests did I have?

The point to be made is that any research is not innocent or objective and is often guided by the subjective questions asked at the beginning and during the research process. Such is the nature of teaching as well.

I discovered in this study that teachers at various points during the day were connected, despite their differences, through their personal struggles to challenge forms of alienation, subordination, and oppression. I learned that curriculum was not necessarily a remote socially efficient entity if teachers commonly viewed themselves as using curriculum to instill in students the creative possibilities of alternative meaning making to their already oppressed existences. In summary, I learned through the three studies that despite differences in time, space, and ideas, possibilities existed to find gaps in the curriculum, the school day, and thought processes, whereby, because of teachers, both teachers and students could become emancipatory change agents that challenged a system that Dewey and other criticalists were or are always challenging.

Certainly, until now, no one consistent method has surfaced in the radical education literature that tells us how to find the "resistant" teacher (or teachers) and/or students. One of the likely reasons for this is that the concept of "resistance" has not been appropriately dealt with. What I propose in the following sections in this chapter then, will be one area of concern in critical educational studies. This area lends insights to other forms of culture that may or may not be "resistant." Thus, what counts as resistance for the radical educational ethnographer, student, and/or teacher is crucial to the everyday world of social transformation. It is to some of the literature and the concept of "resistance" that I now turn.

SOME OF THE LITERATURE

Literature on teacher resistance or accommodation to structural factors in educational fields is sparse. Empirical studies are also far and few between. Theorists such as Aronowitz and Giroux (1985), as well as Wexler (1987) and McLaren (1993, 1994), have carefully scrutinized what teacher resistance does and does not entail. Writers such as Bullough and Gitlin (1985) admit that "the debate over what is resistance and its place in theories of cultural and economic reproduction is a healthy example of critical dialogue, but thus far the empirical work needed to link teacher resistance with emancipatory change is missing" (p. 65). Put differently, they also argue for the need to see how teachers in the everyday world challenge a social efficiency system that merely reproduces and structures inequities. However, Bullough and Gitlin are also limited in their own studies when they choose to focus on one subject (Dave).

In my mind, we need to go further than the one-person case study (as noted, I have been guilty of that too). For instance, one of the key concepts for me in understanding teacher resistance is understanding the structure of group solidarity. How teacher group solidarity functions at the structural level has not been dealt with systematically by critical theorists thus far. They have not looked deeply or systematically enough at how groups of teachers informally conduct power struggles or alternative meaning-making systems and approaches to the stultified socially efficiency-laden sites they are embedded in.

It seems to me that in order to nudge the understanding of teacher resistance further along it is imperative for resistance theorists (which include critical pedagogists) to address the tension that is involved in teacher's lives at the school site, which necessarily has to do with resistance and accommodation to the structural elements of schools. That is, to understand better what resistance may be, one has to understand acts of conformity (accommodation) to the dominant value structures such as excessive individualism, negative forms of competition, race class and gender distortions, and the like, as well as resistance or challenges to undermine these forms of oppressive thinking and acts of behavior. A closer look at the concept of "resistance" will help clarify these comments more.

THE CONCEPT OF RESISTANCE

In order to help clear up the confusion over what resistance consists of, a further distinction between hegemony and counterhegemony is in order. Derived from the Italian Marxist Antonio Gramsci, hegemony refers to the body of practices, energy, lived experiences, or common-sense interpretations that become our unquestioning world. Hegemony, then, refers to an organized assemblage of meanings, wherein the central, effective, and dominant actions are lived. These lived actions contain meanings and values, and constitute the limits of common-sense knowledge. They are part of our consciousness. This common sense is shared meaning, perpetuated in social practice through images and ideas embedded in everyday life.

Common examples of shared meanings can be viewed through media coverage and in areas of aesthetics, such as in art, music, painting, theater and movies. More of this kind of what I term *mind control* can be surmised from various chapters in this book, particularly in Chapter 8 on popular culture. Importantly, it is not one group that deliberately or consciously goes about exerting control over other groups. What results is a kind of control of ideas and values that is not the result of conflict or overt manipulation. Rather, social cohesion is an outcome of hegemony in the generalized adoption of ideas, values, images, and feeling structures by a social collectivity.

It is the power of hegemony that promotes social control and continuity. Researchers have explained how processes of hegemonic control over people's ideas, images, and forms of consciousness result from a prolonged and continuing struggle (Anyon, 1980). They view schooling as a possible socially transformative site in which resistance to cultural reproductive aspects of knowledge, skill, values and attitudes form a "counterhegemony," as the ultimate challenge to forms of alienation, oppression, and subordination, as well as a site for the maintenance and extension of hegemonic understandings.

Two issues must be made clear here. First, counterhegemony can be viewed as a process of meaning making and/or alternative knowledge, which constitutes a possible way out of the reproductive aspects of knowledge. This would include possibilities for teachers, students, or administrators to create a community that speaks to the "good life," which from a critical, pedagogical, theoretical, and practical position means countering forms of oppression, alienation, and subordination, while concurrently searching for a more just building of a social structure. Second, counterhegemony can also ironically be viewed as another way of incorporating resistant groups, such as those represented by the "lads," whom I described a little earlier in this chapter.

Put differently, resistant acts are needed and must be incorporated in social relations for reproduction, accommodation, or conformity to be accomplished. This double view of counterhegemonic or resistant acts has both in the past and at present provided criticalists of education with quite a dilemma. How does one view teachers? Are they passive bearers of a dominant ideology, resistors to structural constraints, both resistors and accommodators, or just one or the other? What are the functions of teachers in the wider social context that do not serve to be merely socially efficient? Are teachers simply pawns in a game manipulated by the state education department, or do teachers have a say in the creation of an alternate system for themselves as well as for their students? If teachers are to be political messengers of sorts, passing on values to students whether consciously or not, an important issue becomes whether these values are linked to a critical endeavor. Or do these values merely exacerbate a socially efficient system built historically on an ideological terrain that spells doom and gloom, one that always moves away from emancipatory hopes, dreams, and possibilities?

Aronowitz and Giroux (1985) have discussed how resistant acts *can* and *are* construed as ambiguous and "may reveal nothing more than an affinity for the logic of domination and destruction" (p. 106). It seems that this may have been the same with my own forms of resistance while growing up. Bullough and Gitlin (1985) as well as myself (1994) have conducted studies on teacher resistance that have to do with the seeds of what could be termed *emancipatory critique*. Resistance in this case has to do with the questioning and interrogating of the dominant ideology. In one of my studies, for instance, resistance had to do with group solidarity. Put differently, individual resistances always endured, yet group resistance, it was argued, exhibited more promise for emancipatory change. Besides, what counted as true acts of resistance was always problematic to grasp. Conceptually, then, what counts as "resistance" is of importance.

Typically there is often much confusion in the critical theory educational literature about resistance as opposed to deviance. I want to clear this up before delving into what I distinguish between *institutional political resistance and cultural political resistance*. Deviance occurs when rules, boundaries, and various sorts of moral classification system lines are crossed. When things do not fit, they are usually labeled as deviant. For instance, putting shoes on the table or having incestuous sex are deviating or deviant acts, and the latter is punishable by law. Both acts involve out-of-place behavior and are threats to original social structures (Wunthrow, Hunter, Bergessen, & Kurzweil, 1984). At best, deviance accommodates rule breakers through a change of rules (e.g., teachers coming late to meetings may be classified as deviant but may argue that the meeting time is poor and there have to be changes). At worst, deviance involves moral irregularities (crime is a typical example). Here, ritual ceremonies (court trials, prisons, death penalty) draw attention to these moral imperfections.

In schools, teachers and administrators often view student behavior as deviant. Thus, students are labeled as discipline problems, hard-core cases, or simply bad kids. As a result, schools have consequences in order to reestablish the moral order—after school and Saturday detention, and so on. In my school days I could have been classified as mildly deviant—coming to class late, not standing in line correctly, chewing gum when this was against the rules, and so on.

Deviance is closely aligned conceptually with institutional political resistance. But, unlike moral irregularities that for example, say, punishable by crime, this kind of resistance involves teachers challenging structural constraints as patterned behaviors. This, like deviance, may also involve the infraction of certain rules, such as having parties in class when one is not supposed to, not standing outside one's classroom door at an appointed time, arriving late to organized meetings for reasons that have to do with one's perception that such events are a waste of time, and questioning and fighting for teacher rights such as access to personal information. This resistance may also encompass a move to more pragmatic curriculum uses rather than following stringent official guidelines, such as teaching a third- or fourth-grade-level English literature lesson to eighth-grade students simply because these students have not yet reached the eighth-grade standard.

Additionally, teachers may withdraw their consent to the teacher-administrator exchange.[1] This may be exhibited, in part, through a particular language code used by teachers that depicts teacher opposition and rule-breaking activities. Here, teachers take it on themselves to flex their muscles so to speak so their voices, both as individuals and possibly as a group, can be felt. In short, teachers better manage their lives at school by engaging in this type of resistance. Unlike deviance, institutional political resistance has deep and organized patterns to it that involve the questioning of school structures (e.g., official curriculum uses, school board policies, etc.), which may be a first and necessary, but not *sufficient,* step leading to

---

[1]Paul Willis, (1977) talks about the notion of consent in terms of teacher-student exchange. That is, an educational exchange revolves around knowledge, skills, values, and attitudes passed on to the student, which in return (or what Willis calls a "fair exchange") the student gives back docility, compliance, and, for the most part, good behavior. If there is a withdrawal of consent, or a challenge to it, much like the lads, cultural codes are broken and the teacher-student relationship redefined. Similarly, within the teacher-administrator exchange, there must be consent given by teachers to the administrators on a moral basis for an exchange to take place and for work to be accomplished. Again, when consent is withdrawn, either through institutional political resistance or what I term in this chapter, cultural political resistance, forms of counterhegemony may be in operation, depending on why and to what ends consent is being withdrawn. See the withdrawal of consent by Ms. Y in one of my studies (Kanpol, 1994, chap. 3), in which she openly challenges administrative sexist attitudes and in so doing denies her consent to the administration to keep quiet and docile and merely follow protocol on very important cultural concerns.

a critical pedagogy, and which in large part is dealing with the attempt to end forms of oppression, alienation, and subordination.

Cultural political resistance should be seen as relatively distinct from institutional political resistance. As transmitters of knowledge to students, teachers can counter the cultural forms that emerge out of the dominant ideology that may lead to the oppression of various peoples (over emphasis on success by basing one's worth purely on achievement, excessive competition, sexism such as female objectification, racism, etc.) only if they question, reflect, and finally, but certainly, *act* on interrogating those patterns. This may involve disseminating curriculum materials so as to raise student's awareness to their own dominated lives, thus opening up possibilities for remodeling student and teacher experiences. This may allow room for new teacher and student codes that could reinvent the nature of authority, a restructuring of curriculum around new experiences that are at variance with older socially efficient models of curriculum stagnation. This form of critique, then, becomes part of the radical notion of resistance that critical pedagogues,for the most part, adopt in different forms as they seek ways to challenge social inequities.

Of course, what constitutes the difference between acts of deviance and/or institutional and cultural resistance may at times seem murky. For instance, to have control over one's job, (Carlson, 1987)—which has to do with institutional political resistance—or for teachers to simply feel alienated (Altenbaugh, 1987), does not necessarily mean that there will be an immediate switch in values (Kanpol, 1994). Job control or simply feeling alienated in one's work does not automatically embrace a reformation of counterhegemonic values, thereby bringing out an alteration in consciousness. The question really lingers: Does job control or just feeling alienated necessarily have to do with a transformation of consciousness to resistance to dominant and oppressive cultural forms? Cultural agency may have something to do with job control and with alienation, but this does not imply automatic movements toward cultural transmutation.

CONCLUSION

It is over forms of institutional political resistance that teachers can begin to foster resistance into the cultural and thereby counterhegemonic terrain. This may be extended by asking questions about institutional political resistance such as: Why is it that I do not like these methods of evaluation? Who controls their formulation? How can I (we) change its format or language so as not to stagnate me (us) into a numerical category or chart? Why is it that we are held accountable for everything we teach? Whose values am I really teaching? How can I (we) change forms of accountability that lead to teachers being more creative in class instead of having teachers daily confront a packaged curricula? How do rules reflect the culture at the school? Who constructs them anyway? Why are they in place? What is their function?

This chapter serves as the tip of the iceberg in the further development on the concept of resistance as a necessary understanding for the roots underlying further critical pedagogical arguments. Any issues that have critical pedagogical elements, such as multiculturalism and gender issues, will necessarily either overtly or covertly deal with resistance as a theoretical device. The role of either the ethnographer, student, and, for our case, the teacher who searches for emancipatory critique is to challenge and end various forms of alienation, oppression, and subordination. This teacher will carefully observe the institutional culture he or she is a part of.

In short, to institutionally resist is only a precursor for liberation *if* and *only if* it can lead to a counterhegemonic form of resistance—what I have termed in this chapter as cultural political resistance. Only by doing so will present and potential critical pedagogues, both theoreticians and practitioners, become more articulate on what counts as resistance as it is reflected in both student and teacher lives within the structure of school and the wider society. As we proceed to the next chapter, I remind readers that the following chapters reflect areas in critical theory or critical pedagogy in education, which in essence sparks different pockets of cultural political resistance.

1. Students must come to an understanding through group work, discussion, and critique, and what constitutes the dominant oppressive values of our society.
   a. Discuss "family values," where values originate from, and what values members of groups live by.
2. On field trips to schools and various classrooms, have students shadow teachers with the intent of learning what values teachers in public schools are teaching.
   a. As an activity, build group work, sharing and discussing how teachers promote or challenge dominant values.
3. Attempt to build a lesson or unit proposal through groups or individually, either through individual subject manner or interdisciplinarily, of what counterhegemony would look like.
   a. A presentation of this proposal to the rest of the students could be a worthwhile activity.

1. Discuss your past school experiences. How did your school reproduce value structures?
   a. Whose values were they and where did they derive from?
   b. Are these values connected to your personal history such as family, etc. If so, how?
2. How have you the student/teacher been hegemonized?
   a. Discuss hegemony in terms of your own particular race, class, and gender constructions, both as an oppressor and the oppressed, the victim and the victimizer, and so on.
3. Have you ever been a deviant? If so how and why.
4. What does cultural political resistance look like to you in the everyday world?
   a. Have you ever felt or been a part of this form of resistance and/or counterhegemony? Describe these instances.
5. How did either your deviance or present institutional political resistance differ to any cultural resistance you may have felt, seen, and/or been a part of?

REFERENCES

Altenbaugh, R. (1987). Teachers at the work place. *Urban Education, 21*(4), 365-389.

Anyon, J. (1980). Social class and the hidden curriculum of work. *Journal of Education, 162,* 66-92.

Aronowitz, S., & Giroux, H. (1985). *Education under siege.* Westport, CT: Bergin & Garvey.

Apple, M. (1979). *Ideology and curriculum.* Boston: Routledge & Kegan Paul.

Apple, M. (1982). *Education and power.* Boston: Routledge & Kegan Paul.

Apple, M., & Weiss, L. (Eds.). (1983). *Ideology and practice in schooling.* Philadelphia: Temple University Press.

Bullough, R., Jr., & Gitlin, A.D. (1985). Beyond control: Rethinking teacher resistance. *Education and Society, 3*(1-2), 65-75.

Carlson, D. (1987). Teachers as political actors. *Harvard Educational Review, 57*(3), 287-309.

Everhart, R. (1983). *Reading, writing and resistance.* Boston: Routledge & Kegan Paul.

Giroux, H. (1983). *Theory and resistance in education.* Westport, CT: Bergin & Garvey.

Hargreaves, A. (1984). Experience counts, theory doesn't: How teachers talk about their work. *Journal of Sociology of Education, 57,* 244-254.

Kanpol, B. (1994). *Critical pedagogy: An introduction.* Westport, CT: Bergin & Garvey.

McLaren, P. (1993). *Teaching as a ritual performance: Toward a political economy of educational symbols and gestures.* New York: Routledge & Kegan Paul.

McLaren, P. (1994). *Life in schools.* New York: Longman.

Shapiro, S. (1990). *Between capitalism and democracy.* Westport, CT: Bergin & Garvey.

Wexler, P. (1987). *Social analysis of education: After the new sociology.* New York: Routledge & Kegan Paul.

Willis, P. (1977). *Learning to labor: How working class kids get working class jobs.* Lexington, MA: D.C. Heath.

Woods, P. (1986). *Inside schools.* New York: Routledge & Kegan Paul.

Wunthrow, R., Hunter, J.D., Bergessen, A., & Kurzweil, E. (1984). *Cultural analysis: The work of Peter Berger, Mary Douglas, Michel Foucault and Jurgen Habermas.* Boston: Routledge & Kegan Paul.

Yeo, F. (1996). *Inner city schools, multiculturalism and teacher education: The search for new connections.* New York: Garland Publishers.

Young, M. (Ed.). (1971). *Knowledge and control.* London: Collier-Macmillan.

PART II

ONGOING TRENDS
IN CRITICAL PEDAGOGY

4

CRITICAL PEDAGOGY AND THE MULTICULTURAL PROJECT

Assistant
Superintendent: Dr. Kanpol, I understand that you conduct curriculum development workshops.

Kanpol: Yes, that is a part of what I can do.

Assistant
Superintendent: What do you think you can offer us here?

Kanpol: Well, I think that a workshop on multicultural education as connected to the curriculum is something that is very important.

Assistant
Superintendent: Oh, we don't need that type of stuff here. We have very few minorities.

ANOTHER CONVERSATION: A PHONE RINGS IN MY OFFICE (1992)

Kanpol: Hello

Woman: Hello, Dr. Kanpol.

Kanpol: Yes

Woman: I was wondering if you could help me.

Kanpol:	Shoot!
Woman:	I am a graduate from this school. I am now a freelance writer. I've been given a 30-day deadline to prepare a workbook on multicultural education by a publishing company. I really don't know much about the topic. I was wondering if you could help.
Kanpol:	Why would you write about something that you aren't familiar with.
Woman:	I guess it's what the market demands.

VIGNETTE (1995)

In a philosophy of education class an in-service student reads a story of Santa and Christmas. Her Santa is African American:

Student:	Multiculturalism is about difference. I would read Christmas stories to students showing that Santa isn't always White.
Kanpol:	You mean to say everyone celebrates Christmas?

INTRODUCTION

The first two conversations represent to me, anyway, a growing logic of despair, particularly around issues of multiculturalism, symbolic of a rising *conservative* trend, in which hegemony is in full force. The assistant superintendent promotes an ethic of ethnocentrism, whereas the "woman" promotes a market logic of consumerism and commodification equated to the ideology of social efficiency. Readers should not be surprised at such logic given social efficiency's history and the general public's lack of intellectual effort to realize the insurmountable problems hegemonic forms of thinking create, particularly around such crucial pedagogical concerns involved in multicultural education. As an example, in my own schooling, I cannot even recall one instance in which one teacher or the curriculum invested in any forms of diversity, let alone challenged forms of "our" or "my" ethnocentrism. This itself was a form of hegemonic control.

For too long now, even school reform (Nation at Risk and Carnegie Report, etc.), especially in the United States, but also abroad, has centered its attention on the need for schools to produce better students, in part, to propel flagging national and international economies. Severely lacking within these reports, however, is serious attention to the mounting social dilemmas with youth (drugs, sex, alcohol, suicide, etc.) and rampant immigration. The issue of educating the immigrant has become a historical fact, as discussed in the first chapter. More importantly however, how to educate and what values to impart are very critical concerns within a democracy. How schools accommodate to more than just celebrating cultural, ethnic, or linguistic diversity in general, but also adjust to social and cultural differences such as race, class, and gender issues, becomes a critical pedagogist's nightmare and is most often ignored by the influential reports as well as suggested by the two introductory conversations. Indeed, the reports have little to say about cultural concerns of the sort mentioned earlier. Yet much is still expected from administrators, teachers, and students in terms of increasing test scores and national averages, despite cultural differences that exist within the schools—all this without a deep understanding of the multicultural problematic.

In a *liberal* sense, schools have begun to promote diversity issues with such activities as increasing minority writers in the curriculum or staging events (such as International Food Day, the celebration of other traditions, etc.). The vignette depicts a liberal mindset—blinded by a view that on the one hand can allow for color difference to define a world of differences, but on the other hand is un-self-critical as well as oblivious to alternate forms of religions or faiths.

With this in mind, and believing that both the conservative and liberal logic can only deepen forms of hegemonic control, I expand, in this chapter, on the "critical" mission of multiculturalism. I attempt this by first briefly elaborating and justifying the incorporation of critical pedagogy and multiculturalism into what has been broadly termed elsewhere as "critical multiculturalism" (Giroux, 1992, 1993; Kanpol & McLaren, 1995). I then outline what five entwined tenets of critical multiculturalism might look like: identity, similarities within differences, popular culture, diaspora that includes home and homelessness, and White supremacy. As a part of my conclusions, I relate these ideas to schools and the multicultural project.

CRITICAL MULTICULTURALISM: SOME OF THE LITERATURE

As has been noted earlier in this book, schools track their students by race, class, and gender, whether overtly or covertly (Anyon, 1980;

McLaren, 1994; Oakes, 1985), through what is often termed the "hidden curriculum."[1] Similarly noted multicultural theorists (Banks, 1994; Darder, 1991; Grant & Sachs, 1995; Sleeter, 1991; Yeo, 1996; and many more) dialogue about the need for integrating a "multicultural" or diverse approach for school curricular in order to foster a more critical and/or egalitarian school climate. These multicultural workers have helped clear the stage to build on difference and voice, "those multifaceted and interlocking sets of meanings through which students and teachers actively engage in dialogue with one another (McLaren, 1994, p. 229).[2]

Multiculturalists ask the education community to expand our view on how, in an economically, socially, and culturally tracked institutionalized school bureaucracy, we can begin to think in grander terms of a multicultural education, as more than just incorporating different voices into the curriculum. They *demand,* in addition, that we view multiculturalism as inclusive of all ethnic voices, which in unity and solidarity speak to and with others in a common and unified bond in an effort to overcome oppressive social and cultural conditions, especially as they pertain to school youth.

With this in mind, Sonia Nieto (1992) has taken up the challenge of theoretically constructing different school voices (varying ethnicities) in her very important work, *Affirming Diversity.* It is no small claim for her to make that "multicultural education" is a process of "comprehensive school reform" (p. 208). As an educational discourse, Nieto has furthered our knowledge of multiculturalism as merely an assimilation process about human relations, democracy or a simple notion of social reconstruction. Nieto has problematized multiculturalism by incorporating it into a part of critical school reform and understanding of those "others" who cross borders (Giroux, 1992) and enter into the terrain of understanding and empathizing with multiply oppressed, alienated, and muted voices (hooks, 1989).

In short, multiculturalism not only affirms diversity and, ultimately, differences, but demands investigation into one's own cultural heritage and individual and group relations to race, class and gender, age and environment, and so on. Aligning multiculturalism with critical pedagogy, then, opens the doors for

---

[1]The hidden curriculum is a term used consistently by critical pedagogists and refers to those unstated values, norms, and attitudes passed to students in their everyday world. Often this involves hegemonically constructed values.

[2]The concept of "voice" is referred to variously throughout this book, and is expanded on later, particularly in Chapter 6.

connections to be made with identity, similarities within differences, popular culture, diaspora, home or homelessness, as well as White supremacy. I now turn to those theoretical and practical problematics as it relates to critical pedagogy and the "critical" multicultural project.

IDENTITY

This is not the place to expand in great detail on the concept of identity. This is a job better completed by other social theorists. I do, however, want to generally allude to identity as it is referred to in multiculturalism. In so doing, I agree with the wisdom of Cornel West (1992), who identifies identity on three levels: conceptually, morally, and politically.

Conceptually, identity, according to West, has to do with desire and death. Desire drives people to attain "recognition, association and protection over time and space" (p. 21). Death occurs because of desire (Julio Rivera, Youseff Hawkins, Martin Luther King) and our inevitable extinction. The crucial link of identity bound within desire and death is hubbed within material resources, land, and labor—in short, who succeeds or not and who competes to establish certain identities.

Desire (the quest to be known) and death (inevitable extinction) bind identity and lead to a moral question: What is the relationship between identity as construed earlier and democracy? How is any person related to the maldistribution of resources or, in the education context, resources related to unequal knowledge, skills, values, and attitudes (cultural capital or Knowledge, Skills, Values, and Attitudes [KSVAs]) that allow any person to succeed or fail with resource attainment? Within the multicultural problematic, the cultures who have access to resource attainment (e.g., cultural capital) becomes a central multicultural concern. How cultures structure desire around personal identity that involves education (cultural capital) is of special significance for critical multiculturalists. The *moral* question of identity, then, will question the democratic nature of multiculturalism. Who attains knowledge? What knowledge is available? Who controls knowledge? These kinds of questions are central to a critical multiculturalist project.

Finally, the political notion of identity has to do with binding people proactively to do something about their present social and cultural condition. A question to ask is: How does one bind, empathize, or become a part of a dominant culture that implies *not to bind*, but to compete tooth and nail for resources (in schools this refers to grades, getting into the top track, competition in its negative senses, etc.)? I argue later that identity as a concept, its moral character and political potential, are entwined with the following four conceptual categories as related to critical multiculturalism.

SIMILARITIES WITHIN DIFFERENCES

A part of identity and "critical multiculturalism" is for teachers and school administrators to come to terms with "difference." It is not enough for school personnel to say that diversity is accepted. Difference as distinct from diversity includes the full range of human subjectivity and thereby touches on individual and group race, class, gender, and age backgrounds, particularly as related to relations of oppression, alienation, and subordination. To understand difference simultaneously means to better understand various cultural histories and social codes (such as mores, norms, and values) without judging them ethnocentrically. Difference, then, is more than just celebrating "International Food Week" like so many schools do, or symbolically including learning about other ethnicities as part of a curriculum. Difference is a serious reconstruction of meaning making about other cultures, especially in relation to one's own culture.

I have argued elsewhere (Kanpol, 1992) that for teachers to understand differences may mean reflecting on a similarity of experiences. For instance, although my Jewish, male, and White experiences may be different, for example, from your Muslim, female, and/or Black experiences, surely in our lives we have "felt" the pain of alienation, oppression, and subordination. Surely, although each individual has different experiences, broadly speaking, I can recount my experiences as an immigrant in Israel, illiterate in the dominant Hebrew language, feeling despair and homeless. Although particular circumstances may differ, the similarities lie in the pain and suffering endured. Hopefully I can better understand a culture through recounting what Sharon Welch (1985) has coined as "dangerous memories," those memories that allow me to understand how I was or am oppressed, thus propelling me to change these conditions. A part of critical multiculturalism, then, is for teachers to construct within their classrooms "similarities within differences," through reflection and memories of experiences.

Identity and multiculturalism is bound within the *desire* to empathize with the "other" (those who are marginalized) as an ongoing relationship of mutual recognition and trust. The moral content and political activism of empathy will allow multiculturalism to flourish in relationships as similarities within differences are explored.

POPULAR CULTURE: YOUTH AND ROCK[3]

Underplayed in the multicultural education literature is the relationship of identity to popular culture. Certainly, desire is connected to popular culture and self-perception within popular culture.

One can view popular culture through a "critical" lens that lends itself to multiculturalism. Particularly, how music forms such as rock or jazz and classical media such as cinema and television relate multiple messages about culture can become a focal point for the teacher to incorporate into his or her critical multicultural approach.

For instance, any multicultural analysis bound within identities will have to take youth seriously in order to understand cultural differences. So telling and problematic is youth's need and acceptance and/or incorporation of musical lyrics into youth consciousness. Frank Zappa (1989) comments on youth relationships to music:

> I think that one of the causes of bad mental health in the United States is that people have been raised on love lyrics. You're a young kid and you hear all those love lyrics, right? Your parents are telling you the truth about love, and you can't really learn about it in school. You're getting the bulk of behavior norms mapped for you in lyrics to some love story. It's a subconscious training that creates a desire for an imaginary situation which will never exist for you. People who buy into that mythology will go through life feeling they got cheated out of something. (pp. 88-89)

On the one hand, rock revels in its challenge to authority. On the other hand, rock represents a "breakdown in the sense of a rational coherent world" (Gergen, 1991, p. 133). Aronowitz (1989) is insightful here, as he relates popular culture (rock as well) to youth struggles:

---

[3]I do a more in-depth analysis on popular culture and its critical import in Chapter 8. It should be noted that popular culture here is used specifically to connect to multiculturalism.

School offers a reward as price for the surrender of the underground culture of the youth community, an exchange which substitutes work and consumption for the pleasures associated with subcultures. Since television and rock music both reinforce these values but also undermine them with the dreams of communal life and sexual pleasure, their reproductive functions are not sufficiently reliable to warrant authoritative approbation. Thus, a pedagogy of popular culture finds itself in the intersistics of the contradictory elements that constitute the forms of the wider society. (p. 202)

Importantly, the message of rock, elaborated by Zappa, Gergen, and Aronowitz, provide the conditions by which it symbolized the struggle over youth identity—the alienation of youth—yet concurrently provides them with the conditions for social and cultural critique.

Rock became an "affective investment"[4] (Grossberg, 1992), a sense of shared public language about different cultures bound within identity. For instance, rap can be viewed as a culture's creation (Black working class in particular, but not limited to only Blacks) of the imprisonment of everyday life, boredom, and surveillance. The relationship of race, class, and gender to rock and asking questions as to why youth "sing so passionately to U2, why they dance so maniacally to Midnight Oil or why they listen so intensely to Fred Frith" (p. 170) may help us understand different cultural relationships to rock and this elusive thing called identity. An important question to ask, which I return to later, would be: Where are there differences and similarities within cultures, as related to student's investments into cultural forms?

YOUTH AND TV AND CINEMA

The struggle over youth as related to critical multiculturalism is also a part of the evolving construction of self and identity, as well as a product of television and cinema. For instance, we can better understand youth culture (and multicultures) by observing the multiple contradictions that project youth images and the *moral* sense of identity that West (1992) eloquently writes about.

---

[4]Affective investment represents the emotional acceptance of particular viewpoints, revolving around values, beliefs, and ideologies. For example, to affectively invest, in the movie *Rocky* is to incorporate, at least in part, excessive competition, the American Dream, and survival of the fittest mentality into one's hegemonic values structure.

Youth is depicted as succumbing to capitalistic virtues (*Family Ties*), nerd (*Pee Wee Herman*), agents of innocence (*Fast Times at Ridgemont High*), the depiction of being number one (*Top Gun*), the spokesman for youth justice (*Pump up the Volume*), the mediator between working- and upper-middle-class life (*Dirty Dancing*), nostalgic (*The Wonder Years*), and also the upcoming Yuppie (*Thirtysomething*).

More than *just* depicting the youth problematic as part of peer culture (school and on the streets) and the domestic culture (home), media portray a serious struggle to redefine different student identities through different cultures. Media define this through challenging youth stereotypes as to what counts as good looking (*MASK*), which ethnicity can be successful at school (*Stand and Deliver*), and a clash of school racial cultures that finds some modicum of harmony (e.g., Black and White as in *To Sir with Love*).

All these suggest that youth and identity are represented in multiple (often similar, yet also different) contradictory forms. On the one hand, then, media represent a hegemonic function that articulates the common desires and interests of the culture (success as defined in the *Cosby* show), survival of the fittest in a competitive society (*LA Law*), capitalism (*Family Ties*), cut-throat competition, hard-work ethic, success as the number one motivator (*Stand and Deliver*), patriarchy (*Archie Bunker* and *The Jeffersons*), and racial stereotypes (*Do the Right Thing, Color Purple*).

These suggest that media colonize identity patterns. Yet, concurrently, media also represents moments of struggle over the moral nature of identity. Democracy and the family (*Family Ties*), incorporation of the oppressed class as part of a legitimate struggle for fair rights for different ethnic groups (*Stand and Deliver*), and understanding multiple personality identities (*Pump up the Volume*) all suggest that what will count as youth "critical multicultural identity" opens up the multicultural problematic to a far greater degree than any educational reports deal with. Yet another aspect of critical multiculturalism that needs exploring is the "diaspora and home/homelessness" dialectic.

DIASPORA AND HOME/HOMELESSNESS

The notion of "diaspora" is one alluded to, particularly by minority writers. Simply, diaspora refers to the continued displacement, alienation, and despair that any set of people have within their social

and cultural institutional place of existence. Pessimistically, to be in
the diaspora is to consciously and unconsciously recreate
hopelessness in one's personal, social, and cultural condition.
Diaspora, then, may assume hegemonic consumption, false
consciousness, or the colonization of identity to be something that one
is not or does not necessarily want to be (e.g., to assume the traits
engulfed by White middle-class culture). Within the diaspora,
colonized sensibilities fuel the dominant ideology and a reification of,
for instance, White, male, and Wasp cultural homogeneity. In large
part, the concept of diaspora produces within minority cultures "the
problem of invisibility and namelessness . . . a quest for validation
and recognition on the ideological, social and cultural terrains of non-
minorities" (West, 1992, pp. 26-27). The crisis of identity for
minorities, then, seems to rest in *getting out* of the diaspora, a place
of *homelessness*, and finding their own capacity for self-identification,
authenticity, alignment of history to the present, reflection on past
subordination, alienation, and oppression to a sense of feeling at
home, both outside and inside the dominant culture—to be border
crossers as Giroux (1992) points out. Put differently, *home*, unlike
homelessness, represents a re-representation of self and identity that
is constantly grappling with a sense of doubt or a sense of double
consciousness (a movement between the authentic self within one's
own history and culture and the dominant culture one is accepting or
even questioning). The crisis of identity, as West (1992) and hooks
(1989) discuss, is bound within the diasporic notion of home and
homelessness and what counts as self within dominant cultures.

      In schools, the problematic of diaspora and home and
homelessness is of central concern for a critical multiculturalism.
That is, to simply celebrate a culture by announcing that one believes
in diversity, for instance, is not necessarily to achieve a sense of
authenticity about a counterhegemonic consciousness. Partying
"International Food Week" will not guarantee a sense of home and
authentic identity. Possibly a school's ability to assume what West
calls a prophetic wisdom that appropriates a cultural politics of
difference and that is partisan to deconstructing what cultures have
historically meant (their struggles, alienation, subordination, and
oppression) can lead to insight, pleasures, and challenges of
understanding and meaning about different cultures. Put another
way, within schools, for critical multiculturalism to appear,
difference (and its multiplicities) must be challenged head on in order
to gain a sense of authenticity and home. Forms of media must be
scrutinized. Music must be interrogated. Cultures must be
demystified. History has to be read and reread with a magnifying

glass. Art history must be understood within their different cultural contexts. Social studies classes must be used as a vehicle for critique. In short, critical multicultural teachers must begin to also interrogate their own cultural stereotypes as related to similar and different student cultures and biases.

This challenge requires teachers to "look at" multiculturalism as more than a mere structural challenge—but as a visionary and existential challenge of freedom within relentless deconstruction. Only then can the diaspora be seen for what it is, and home can become a reality.

WHITE SUPREMACY

Connected to the diaspora and living in it is the notion of *White supremacy*. White supremacy assumes that dominant social and at times oppressive values become the organizing factor around which schools operate through the hidden curriculum. Although much of this has been documented elsewhere (Anyon, 1980; Apple, 1979, 1986; Britzman, 1992; Giroux, 1992; Kanpol, 1992; McLaren, 1994; Oakes, 1985; Willis, 1977; Yeo, 1996; among many others) deconstructing Whiteness within the school site (and obviously outside of this site) is to take multiculturalism to its most critical heights. Simply, critical multiculturalism takes on a political spectrum, one that simultaneously is critical of "Whiteness" as well as of any other culture that accepts Whiteness as the only legitimate dominant form.

In short, the critical and political sides of multiculturalism are entwined within a multicultural political democracy. Critical multiculturalism, then, is ultimately tied to a democratic ideal or a "democratic imaginary" (Laclau & Mouffe, 1985), those acts that work to alleviate any sense of oppression, subordination, and alienation in personal and professional (teachers in this case) lives. Marable (1992) is worth quoting here:

> Multicultural political democracy means that this country was not built by and for only one group—Western Europeans; that our country does not have only one language—English; or only one religion—Christianity; or only one economic philosophy—corporate capitalism. Multicultural democracy means that the leadership within our society should reflect the richness, colors and diversity expressed in the lives of all people. Multicultural democracy demands new types of power-sharing and the re-allocation of

resources necessary to great economic and social development for
those who have been systematically excluded and denied. (Marable,
1992, p. 13)

Closely aligned to this democratic notion is the ability for
teachers and students as all other school personnel to deconstruct
their own color, irrespective of Whiteness. I use Whiteness as a
marker, however, because of the inevitable hegemonic Whiteness-
type inclusion into the mainstream. Identity, then, is bound within
the "Whiteness" critique. Self and other are inextricably bound
within whiteness. Media and art are connected to Whiteness. And,
finally, similarity within differences is intimately connected to
Whiteness. Only when symbols of Whiteness are critically
deconstructed (through values, metaphors, holidays, etc.) will critical
multiculturalism become a force within schools.

CONCLUSION

I return to the notion that in order for schools to incorporate and
affectively invest into a critical multiculturalism, as part of a critical
pedagogy movement, deconstruction of multiple aspects of cultures
must take place. In large part, this form of education is decidedly
political. Although Aronowitz and Giroux (1994) are correct in saying
that in order for teachers to become what they describe as
"transformative intellectuals," they must make the political more
pedagogical and the pedagogical more political for schools to ever
hope of being sites where equality is practiced. Even more than this,
the political notion of multiculturalism must as West (1992) so ably
describes also be a "challenge principally consisting of forging solid
and reliable alliances of people of color and white progressives guided
by a moral and political vision of greater democracy and individual
freedom in communities and states" (p. 24).

Bound within identity, then, critical multiculturalism in
schools as elsewhere begs the questions: What is the moral content of
one's cultural identity? How do we desire it? What are the political
consequences of this moral content and cultural identity? And how do
we, as Giroux brilliantly argues, theoretically and practically account
for border crossings, where identities are meshed within similarities
and differences as well as various modernistic, postmodern, and
feminist tenets, among other theoretical frameworks.

Only with this scrutiny will critical multiculturalism and
critical pedagogy unite theoretically as well as practically in their

quest for a more just and equitable society. The terrain of struggle is to carve out new and emerging identities as part of a critical multicultural project.

1. In groups discuss how or if stereotypes of other ethnicities were formulated as you were growing up.
2. In various subject groups, describe both generally and or in detail, through lesson or unit plan, how the voices of the alienated and oppressed could best be represented in the curriculum.
3. Now in different subject area groups, with say three or four different subjects represented, discuss how the critical multicultural education project would look like interdisciplinarily.
4. On field experiences, both out of school, but perhaps more likely in school, note "difference."
   a. Discuss differences as related to dress, language, and behavior.
5. You are a teacher in a conservative area of the country. You believe in a critical multicultural approach to education. You have to convince people (teachers and principal) of its importance. Construct a justificatory letter explaining your position.
6. You are now the principal of a school and you believe in a more progressive/critical multicultural approach. Where do you even start to reconstruct teachers' ideas? How would the school day be organized?

1. What values were instilled into you regarding difference?
2. Was difference considered in your schooling experiences?
3. How was difference reinforced and/or denied a voice?
4. What did your curriculum look like growing up and/or where you are teaching now regarding various forms of multiculturalism (paying lip service, etc.)?
5. How have you been hegemonized into "White supremacy?"

6. Where have you felt alienated, oppressed and/or subordinated, both in and out of school?
7. What would a "resistant" multicultural curriculum look like?

REFERENCES

Anyon, J. (1980). Social class and the hidden curriculum of work. *Journal of Education, 162,* 66-92.

Apple, M. (1979). *Ideology and curriculum.* New York: Routledge & Kegan Paul.

Apple, M. (1986). *Teachers and texts.* New York: Routledge & Kegan Paul.

Aronowitz, S. (1989). Working class identity and celluloid fantasies in the electronic age. In H. Giroux & R. Simon (Eds.), *Popular culture, schooling and everyday life* (pp. 197-218) Westport, CT: Bergin & Garvey.

Aronowitz, S., & Giroux, H. (1994) *Education still under siege.* Westport, CT: Bergin & Garvey.

Banks, J. (1994). *Multiethnic education.* Boston: Allyn & Bacon

Britzman, D. (1992). *Practice makes practice.* New York: State University of New York Press.

Darder, A. (1991). *Culture and power in the classroom.* Westport, CT: Bergin & Garvey.

Gergen, J.K. (1991). *The saturated self.* New York: Basic Books.

Giroux, H. (1992). *Border crossings.* New York: Routledge.

Giroux, H. (1993). *Living dangerously.* New York: Lang.

Grant, C., & Sachs, J. (1995) Multicultural education and postmodernism: Movement toward a dialogue. In B. Kanpol & P. McLaren (Eds.), *Critical multiculturalism: Uncommon voices in a common struggle* (pp. 89-106). Westport, CT: Bergin & Garvey.

Grossberg, L. (1992). *We gotta get out of this place.* New York: Routledge.

hooks, b. (1989). *Talking back.* Boston: South End Press.

hooks, b. (1991). *Breaking bread.* Boston: South End Press.

Kanpol, B. (1992). *Towards a theory and practice of teacher cultural politics: Continuing the postmodern debate.* Norwood, NJ: Ablex.

Kanpol, B., & McLaren, P. (Eds.). (1995). *Critical multiculturalism: Uncommon voices in a common struggle.* Westport, CT: Bergin & Garvey.

Laclau, E., & Mouffe, C. (1985). *Hegemony and the socialist strategy.* London: Verso.

Marable, M. (1992). *Black America: Multicultural democracy in the age of Clarence Thomas and David Duke.* Westfield, NJ: Open Media.

McLaren, P. (1994). *Life in schools.* New York: Longman.

Nieto, S. (1992). *Affirming diversity.* New York: Longman.

Oakes, J. (1985). *Keeping track: How schools structure inequality.* New Haven, CT: Yale University Press.

Sleeter, C. (Ed.). (1991) *Empowerment through multicultural education.* Albany: State University of New York Press.

Welch, S. (1985). *Communities of resistance and solidarity.* New York: Orbis Press.

West. C. (1992). A matter of life and death. *October, 61,* 20-28.

Willis, P. (1977). *Learning to labor: How working class kids get working class jobs.* Lexington, MA: D.D. Heath.

Yeo, F. (1996). *Inner city schools, multiculturalism and teacher education: The search for new connections.* New York: Garland Press.

Zappa, F. (1989). *The real Frank Zappa story.* New York: Poseidon.

5

A CONTRADICTION OF TEACHER PROFESSIONALISM: A GENDER CRITIQUE

I recall vividly my teacher training program in Israel (which, I may add, was not very different from the ones I taught in Ohio, North Carolina, California, and Pennsylvania). I was preparing to become an English language and literature teacher. Luckily, unlike other prospective teachers who were in training with me, I stumbled across employment in a high school that was in urgent need of an English teacher replacement for its 9th- and 11th-grade English language and literature classes. So the real world of teaching with various discipline problems, different student learning styles, the hustle and bustle of a busy teacher schedule, and so on hit me while still a preservice teacher enrolled in Tel Aviv University's teacher education program.

There is no doubt in my mind that I was what could be described as a snotty know-it-all. I was determined that it was going to be difficult to teach me how to teach within the teacher education program because I perceived myself to be talented and already involved in the battlefield of discipline and the reality of teaching kids who did not really want to be at school. Yet, through my initial stubbornness and know-it-all attitude, I was privy to two very important and central facts. First, there was a major difference between (a) what teacher educators were saying school was about, (b) state-mandated curricular guidelines handed to me, and (c) what actually went on within the four walls of the classroom. Fortunately, or unfortunately, as a prospective teacher I saw through these basic contradictions—and it bothered me greatly. Second, I was receiving the message from my professors that one had to be nurturing, caring, and compassionate to be an effective teacher. One also had to be a good listener and make sure that all children were taught to the best of their ability—all kids could and should succeed (of course, this was fed to me irrespective of social class and general inequities in the "real" world) was a central message I received.

Yet, contradictorily, I believed, I was being taught to teach in very mechanical (this is the only way to do it approach) and robotic ways. For instance, lesson and unit plans were standardized—only certain descriptive words could be used for behavioral objectives. Teaching methods taught were not flexible. The professor's way was the right way. Was this a social efficiency mind-set again that I was experiencing?

To cut a long story short, I struggled through the teacher education program, realizing that rigidity was the order and structure so profound that any deviating from it would be considered blasphemy. Despite all the "females" that went to school with me (I was one of two males in a class of 30 prospective English teachers), something else was going on in teacher education that left me gasping. I was to finish the certification program as a "professional" armed with the tools to supposedly both survive and succeed as a teacher. I have since my days as a student in this particular program and my critical theory studies realized that the issues I described earlier are really gender related. I want to clarify one very important fact. When I talk about gender here, I do not necessarily mean only male or female, but I refer to a particular technocratic or social efficient mindset that can be within any male or female.

With that in mind, my aim in this chapter is to connect some issues of "gender" through the lens of the critical theory literature in education to the professionalism of teachers. I first look at some of this literature as it applies to teacher and gender relations, a teacher contradictory position, and teacher professionalism. I then respond to three questions: What is the immediate impact of this contradiction in the school and how could teachers deal with it? What can the administrator (principal) do to deal with this contradiction? Why is it necessary to understand these contradictions?

SOME OF THE CRITICAL LITERATURE ON TEACHERS AND GENDER

Critical social theorists in education (Giroux & McLaren, 1989; hooks, 1994; Kanpol, 1994; McLaren, 1994) have argued that schools are sites of profound cultural struggles. Within these struggles gender relations in particular have been viewed primarily as a function of ongoing oppression. Supporting this argument is the view that a part of female teacher oppression involves the sexual division of labor in the school. This has been historically constructed (Connell, 1985; Connell, Ashenden, Kessler & Dowsett, 1982; Tyack & Hansot, 1988) and impacts schools in various ways (Ginsburg, 1987). To Apple (1986) the division of labor at schools lies between images of patriarchy and matriarchy. Apple is worth quoting at length:

> Patriarchal familial forms in concert with changes in the social division of labor of capitalism combine here to create some of the conditions out of which a market for a particular kind of teacher emerges. (p. 62) While women struggled to open up the labor market and later patriarchal relations in the home and in the paid workplace, some of the arguments used for opening up teaching to women . . . the relationship between teaching and domesticity was highlighted. (p. 63)

Put in a slightly different way, women teachers, he argues, have been oppressed because of their socially constructed stereotype—naturally empathetic, caring, and responsive to rules—thus making them ideally suited for teaching and the marketplace, where punctuality and control were or are dominant values. Apple contends that this among other reasons has denied women equal pay, as well as the autonomy and control of their teaching occupation. Men, on the contrary, teacher or administrator, are seen as natural authoritarians or strict disciplinarians. It is precisely this form of stereotype that depicts an area of a cultural struggle between gender images that critical pedagogues have long struggled with. Comment Myra Strober and David Tyack (1980):

> By structuring to take advantage of sex role stereotypes about women's responsiveness to rules and male authority, and men's presumed ability to manage women, urban school boards were able to enhance their ability to control curricula, students and personnel . . . difference of gender provided an important form of social control. (p. 499)

Just as in my teacher training program, the imagery of mastery and control as well as social efficiency was a metaphor for gender relations construction in which it did not matter as to a person's particular gender. What mattered most were the traits, values, attitudes, and beliefs being taught to prospective teachers. They emanated from a stereotype, historically constructed, around what the theorists just quoted have described as being dominated by a male hegemonic form of thinking.

What has been largely ignored in the literature on teachers, however, is how these gender relations can be turned around to be viewed as a source of affirmation and possibility, not only oppression. While Apple's argument is important, it is, in my mind, too simple an analysis for understanding the tensions of teachers' (both male and female) lives. This has some very important and critical ramifications.

TEACHER CONTRADICTORY GENDER POSITIONS

I begin this section by enhancing Apple's thesis. Teachers in general (rather than predominantly women teachers in the main he argues) face a complex (perhaps postmodern), contradictory identity confusion. This involves a stereotypical gender role that at first depicts the teacher acting as nurturer on the one hand and classroom manager on the other. The former holds that teachers be caring, empathetic, loving, in communion, or part of a communion. This, in part, depicts the image of the historically constructed female gender image. The latter indicates that teacher be agentic—decisive, in control, objective, authoritarian, task-oriented, assertive, and so on (Bakan, 1966). This also, historically constructed, becomes the male stereotype.

With these gender distinctions in mind, teachers pass to their students a confusing message, typified by a language, behavior, and attitude code that contains this dual consciousness. More subtly, teachers may use this stereotype to structure their social relations. This point has been made or at least implied and substantiated by my many feminist theorists (Daly, 1973; Dodson-Grey, 1982; Gilligan, 1982; hooks, 1994; Noddings, 1992; Welch, 1985; among many others) who argue that "male" ways of thought permeate consciousness so deeply that they deny women and people in general an alternate language to express themselves, a criticality described by Aronowitz and Giroux (1985) as a "language of possibility," one that searches for a way out of hegemonic thinking structures.

To be sure, many feminists both within and outside the school of education are cognizant of gender distinctions. They are endeavoring to cultivate a language that speaks to human liberation—away from oppressive male and female language and thought codes (Noddings, 1992). What these feminists sometimes fail to admit, however, is that *all* people seem to contain this contradictory consciousness elaborated on earlier. This form of consciousness has an immediate impact on teachers and what is generally described in the education field as teacher professionalism.

GENDER AND PROFESSIONALISM

Much of the literature in the education journals focuses on the question of what gender traits it takes to be a "professional." One could take the stance that to be a "professional" requires the acquisition of certificates, the meritocratic notion of success and achievement. It seems to me that what has been valorized is precisely the "male stereotype" in defining the professional. To be a professional, then, one must be in control, autonomous, adhere to the letter of the law, and be a scientific master, in short, be the bearer of a social efficiency mindset. Bledstein's (1976) comments, in this case, are insightful:

> Far more than any other type of society, democratic ones require pervasive symbols of authority, symbols that a majority of people could reliably believe just and warranted. It became the function of schools in America to legitimize the authority of the middle classes (and elites) by appealing to the universality and objectivity of "science." (pp. 123-124)

Thus, the professional could be stereotyped as the person who is objective, a disciplinarian, managerial, and detached. The stereotype could also include the warm, attached teacher, in which the "images of hierarchy and web, drawn from the texts of men's and women's fantasies and thoughts, convey different views on morality and self" (Gilligan, 1982, p. 62). This understanding of the dual nature of professionalism leaves future as well as present teachers in a particular moral bind. How do teachers find a middle path between their professional activities as jeopardizing their own sense of themselves, given their contradictory gender stereotype? Clearly, there is no one answer to this difficult question.

THE IMMEDIATE IMPACT OF THIS CONTRADICTION

Within the perplexing bind teachers can find themselves in, educational critical theorists have long argued that dominant thought modes embody what they variously describe as a "technocratic rationality," serving to encourage conformity to the status quo and minister to the interests of others who benefit from such acquiescence (Beyer & Zeichner, 1987; Giroux, 1980; Popkewitz, 1987). Put differently, this technocratic mindset is clearly one in which ideas and action as well as the embodiment of dominant values becomes all pervasive, much like a social efficiency model of reasoning. Thus, a stultified set of attitudes, values, and behaviors have all too often become part of both the teachers' as well as teacher education's world. This has led to sterility in thinking about teacher professionalism in more than just one "modern" (rational, logical) way (Yeo, 1996).

I argue that to understand the gender contradiction outlined previously and to "act" critically one will begin to lay the groundwork to "resist" the status quo of conforming or accommodating to only one particular stereotype and, at least in part, challenge teacher education's sterility. This may manifest itself in numerous ways. What follows is the beginning of a platform that discusses two of the immediate impacts that a gender "understanding" may have on teacher professionalism: (a) taking a stance over policy, and (b) remodeling the purpose of curriculum.

Take a stance over policy issues that exhibit the qualities of both the male and female stereotype. An example might help here. In a recent study of mine (Kanpol, 1994), two female teachers wrote a letter of complaint to the administration of their school and district questioning a sexual assault charge concerning two boys who had assaulted one of their common female students. These teachers, as a part of the eighth-grade teaching staff, were made aware of this occurrence two months after the event. They needed to act swiftly, be disciplined, managerial, and detached when constructing a letter to the administration, which had policy ramifications. Quite possibly, this typified the image of the male stereotype. What informed the decision to write the letter, however, was precisely these two teachers' agentic, connected self, and attached qualities that depicted the image of the female stereotype.

What seems obvious in this scenario is that the teacher contradictory gender "position" laid the framework for questioning and acting to change policy. The professional teacher in this scenario, then, was viewed as *distanced* when constructing the letter for higher authorities (such as the principal and superintendent), but *caring* and *connected* about the incident that informed such a writing.

A redefinition of the purpose of curriculum takes many forms. In large part, teachers today are held more accountable for students' test scores, use both a standardized and a detached curriculum (such as a curriculum that is not connected to personal experiences), as well as administer objective and depersonalized tests. Teachers are also subject to dehumanizing evaluative rating scales. This form of pedagogy can only be "resisted" when the issues of control and detachment over curriculum items is questioned and acted on in the caring and nurturing qualities of an alternate image than the previous one. Thus, to reject a curriculum that avoids interactive and involved dialogue between teachers and students over social concerns such as prejudice, race, sex, and age discrimination will indirectly and hegemonically reinforce schools as sterile environments or socially efficient and thus promote a technocratic mindset. Critical pedagogy challenges this form of rationality head on with the intent to obliterate stereotypes that oppress, alienate, and subordinate others into mechanistic thinkers.

To begin to question these issues can take many twists and turns. In economic classes there can be simulations on "buying power," "supply and demand," and "fiscal policy." In math classes, "shopping" or learning to balance a checkbook can become a personalized issue. In social studies classes, topics of "prejudice" such as in "race" and "social class" as well as "gender" issues can predominate. In language arts classes, the issues of "time, characterization, and place" are usually talked about. All these topics begin in some way to help one see how the world is divided by gender in unfair and manipulative ways. Who does the shopping? Who controls fiscal policy? Who writes the checks? Who's prejudiced? Where's your time, characterization, and place? How does it relate to yours and others' experiences?

Questioning and subsequent dialogue of this nature begins to redefine the teacher as professional, as both the *authority* in terms of knowledge and hierarchy (notice, not the authoritarian) and also as *attached* in terms of social commitment. Here, student worth will be based on their humanity and their uniqueness, rather than their immediate achievements or accomplishments. Underlying this pedagogical rubric, teachers can practice *creativity, dialogue,* and *subjectivity* rather than *stagnation* and *objectivity,* in which the ultimate concern becomes connectedness, relating a sometimes stagnant, socially efficient model of standardized curriculum to the pragmatics of experience and interests, in the most fundamental, nurturing, and critical sense. Amazingly, what I have argued for are good reasons for prospective teachers to become teachers, why perhaps some even do. Somewhere, however, in the hustle and bustle of the everyday world of a public school, these images are swallowed up by a social efficiency ideology.

It could be argued that the teacher as professional is often trapped within the gender stereotype. To be able to move between its polarities, both affirming and concurrently negating one or the other stereotype, would be an initial step to help redefine what the function of the curriculum is. Certainly, to interrogate the overt (official) curriculum in such a manner begins to lay the foundations for further dialogue, critique, exploration, reflection, and, finally, a redefinition of the teacher professional role in the social order.

In short, teachers as professionals, as described earlier, possess the political potential to reject and disrupt a "given" state of society. An affirmation that this rejection of either stereotype as the dominating one may lead to a liberating-type language (or a form of counterhegemony), in which social relations are redefined. In many of her works, Kristeva reminds us that women face the challenge of *balancing* gender images. I argue that any teacher (male or female) faces this difficult challenge, in which a new and just social order based on equality, care, and nurturance becomes a language of possibility. The task related to administrators and as seen in the earlier light is not an enviable one. It is a task, however, that is needed to offset at least a stereotypical image of gender in the teaching profession, which often leads to various forms of alienation, oppression, and subordination.

WHAT CAN THE ADMINISTRATOR (PRINCIPAL) DO TO DEAL WITH THIS CONTRADICTION?

The principal has also been described by me elsewhere as one who embodies various contradictions (Kanpol, 1989, 1991), as embodying more than one "voice." It must be understood that, in large part, the principal, too, represents the image of the contradictory male and female stereotype (e.g., detached authoritative decision maker vs. the caring humanist and one who is in communion).

Although there is abundant literature on what counts as effective leadership (Baily & Adams, 1990; Lewellen, 1990; Peterson,

1985; Snyder & Johnson, 1985), my purpose is not to list these qualities. For me, this becomes too technical. What is important, however, is to understand the role the principal can play as a leader in moving between the image of the gender contradiction. This is part of a critical understanding of a school leader's role, more of which is dealt with in a later chapter.

The nature of administrator, decision maker, evaluator, rule and policy maker and keeper, organizer of induction programs, or promoter of extracurricula activities must begin to be defined through the contradictory gender image discussed earlier, as at least a starting point for a counterhegemonic/resistant possibility. This would look like an administrator impulse that speaks to both male and female stereotypical gender structures—a praxis loaded with justice and care, representing both principles and standards as well as connectedness.

At the outset, to effectively deal with these contradictions, the principal must find a fine balance between gender roles. First, a necessary step by principals to effect emancipatory change based on this contradiction begins with an understanding that "literacy" is not only a concept that deals with reading, writing, and computing skills; rather, literacy or to be literate means to be able to understand and interpret the social world from multiple levels. To simply promote *functional* literacy and/or *cultural* literacy (understanding one's and other's culture) is not necessarily interrogative or a critical stance of one's own complicitous identity and personhood in social relationships, particularly about gender issues. Thus, a striving for a *critical literacy* is a necessary condition for both the critical pedagogical teacher and principal, particularly if one wants to interrogate the contradiction of the sort mentioned in this chapter.

Second, *dialogical* decision making versus *authoritative* and swift decision making can help promote a critical literacy, which I further define as a critical reading of the world. This, of course, translates into principals letting go of total authority and affirming teachers' sense of professional judgment over the decision-making process, a sense of teachers being and showing their own forms of literacy. This necessitates that the principal does *not* become *just* a facilitator of decisions, but an active participant in the construction *with* teachers. Of course, open dialogue means hard-nosed realities, which may also include both teachers and even principals speaking out vulnerably on their own senses of oppression, alienation, and subordination.

Third, evaluation speaks to teacher *subjective input* through *negotiation* versus cold *objective* evaluation and *nonnegotiation*. This translates into principals' understanding more of what occurs in teacher classes, so as to better *sympathize* and *empathize* with the teacher. Only by doing so will any negotiation on content and/or method of teaching take place.

Fourth, policy decisions are necessary that are teacher dialogued and eventually created versus policy decisions that are merely executed as someone else's goals. This involves promoting teacher creativity as part of a shared school community, as opposed to allowing teachers to become only individual acting members of the school as well as puppets of the local and state government.

Fifth, the principal must promote teacher worth and dignity—a fundamental sense of sharing and praising teacher individuality (praising who one is) versus fostering a competitive climate that renders individualism (the emphasis on praising only what one achieves). Discussion on what effects of *merit* pay are versus jealousy over who gets the "extra buck" could be necessary. Informed, genuine, and heart-felt criticism of teachers by peers and administrators guides teacher worth and dignity.

Finally, *any* other action that has at its base a foundation of human nurturance and tolerance rather than detachment and stagnation (as readers will note, much like a social efficiency model) is also important. These actions can range from morning greetings, to school personnel, to discipline measures, to mixing with students on the playground and in the lunch halls and with teachers during their lunch period. This also includes nurturance and tolerance concerning student discipline measures as well as the critical issues of tenure decisions concerning teachers.

CONCLUSIONS: WHY UNDERSTAND THE CONTRADICTIONS

The only slightly related gender issues elaborated on in this chapter appeal to both teachers and principals (as well as other school administrators) to join together to appropriately flux between the image of the male and female gender stereotype, necessary for what Lyons (1983) calls a "morality of justice" and a morality of "response and care" (p. 136). This *dual* existence indeed represents a cultural struggle over gender relations as it is reflected in the school as well as a potential counterhegemonic possibility.

If this struggle is to be taken seriously, I believe that this will ultimately involve breaking "new ground" at school sites, at which adhering to unique ways of decision and policy making takes into account the social relations of gender struggles, both at the practical and symbolic levels. In a sense, then, this struggle also takes on political ramifications, all the while carving out a discourse of new and revitalized values and attitudes. To even attempt this struggle becomes a novel approach to a stultified social efficiency, technocratic system. For this reason, understanding this gender contradiction (as well as others, of course) may allow both principals and teachers in a *nonbureaucratic* leadership style to strive for a leadership that leads to "efficacy rather than accountability, teacher empowerment rather than principal control, flexibility rather than rigidity and facilitation rather than intervention" (Bailey & Adams, 1990, p. 27).

To speak of the division of gender at school only is but the tip of the iceberg, but nevertheless a very important and necessary step by critical pedagogists to better understand social relations as related to peoples who are oppressed, alienated, and subordinated, be they male or female, majority or minority. To gain further ground in this area, new avenues of thought—interpretative, critical, and evaluative—will have to combine with a very real possibility of what it takes to make these conditions available. Put differently, perhaps I as a critical pedagogue have taken just one step by naming a contradiction that is gender related and suggested ways to deal with this contradiction.

I would like to see, however, more research by field-based critical pedagogists (critical ethnographers) that struggle with these gender issues in similar, yet emergingly creative ways. For instance, there are many excellent feminist analyses of schools in the critical educational literature today. Nel Noddings (1992) is constructing an ethic of care. bell hooks (1994) seriously engages her own African-American voice as an example of oppression, but uses that voice to "talk back" and challenge oppressive social forms. Beverly Gordon (1995), similarly a Black female educator, calls for dialogue between various feminists to challenge their own authoritarian voice, their own domination. Other feminists such as Lather (1991) and Ellsworth (1989) seriously call for challenging our own socially constructed thought processes. The list goes on and on.

With this in mind, only theory making such as the kind I have suggested, combined with the reality of lived conditions, will allow for a language and struggle of affirmation, hope, joy, and possibility for student, teacher, and administrator at the school site. Only then can we begin to acquire a better handle of such slippery concepts as "professionalism."

---

1. On field trips to schools list (a) the division of labor as you see it, or (b) the "mindsets" of teachers regarding "social efficiency" versus challenges to this viewpoint.
   a. Discuss in class how these stereotypes lead to student learning and the general classroom climate.
2. In your lesson and unit plans, identify the stereotypical qualities discussed in this chapter.
   a. Justify to yourselves and classmates why you use them.
3. As a form of reflection, dialogue in groups how this particular class and/or this particular teacher represents the stereotypical images outlined earlier.
   a. Suggest ways that the instructor may improve his or her teaching based on this discussion.

---

1. Discuss your family life as indicative of gender roles?
   a. Were things at home fair or not?
2. How was your schooling typical of the male-female stereotypes?
   a. Did this effect your learning, and, if so, how?
   b. How was the curriculum portrayed—socially efficient (mechanistic, predictable, etc.) or more creative?
3. How were personal relationships conducted both in and out of school?
   a. What were the rules or norms governing behavior, etc.? How can this be connected to gender stereotypes?
   b. Were these expectations inhibiting at all? How?
4. Discuss potential topics in your curriculum usage reflective of counterhegemonic forms of thinking regarding the contradictions mentioned in this chapter.
5. Discuss your university experiences relative to the contents of this chapter.

REFERENCES

Apple, M. (1986). *Teachers and texts.* New York: Routledge and Kegan Paul.

Aronowitz, S., & Giroux, H. (1985). *Education under siege.* Westport, CT: Bergin & Garvey.

Bailey, G., & Adams, W. (1990, March). Leadership strategies for non-bureaucratic leadership. *NASSP,* pp. 21-28.

Bakan, D. (1966). *The duality of human existence.* Boston: Beacon Press.

Beyer, L., & Zeichner, K. (Eds.). (1987). Teacher education in cultural context: Beyond reproduction. In *Critical studies in teacher education* (pp. 316-334). New York: Falmer Press.

Connell, R. (1985). *Teacher's work.* Boston: George Allen Unwin.

Connell, R.W., Ashendon, D.J., Kessler, S., & Dowsett, G.W. (1982). *Making the difference.* Sydney: George Allen Unwin.

Daly, M. (1973). *Beyond God the father: Towards a philosophy of women's liberation.* Boston: Beacon Press.

Dodson-Grey, E. (1982). *Patriarchy as a conceptual trap.* Wellesley, MA: Roundtable Press.

Ellsworth, E. (1989). Why doesn't this feel empowering? Working through the repressive myths of critical pedagogy. *Harvard Educational Review, 59*(3), 297-324.

Gilligan, C. (1982). *In a different voice.* Cambridge, MA: Harvard University Press.

Ginsburg, M. (1987). Reproduction, contradiction and conceptions of professionalism: The case of pre-service teachers. In T. Popkewitz (Ed.), *Critical studies in teacher education* (pp. 86-129). New York: Falmer Press.

Giroux, H. (1980). Teacher education and the ideology of social control. *Journal of Education, 162*(11), 5-27.

Giroux, H., & McLaren, P. (Eds.). (1989) *Critical pedagogy, the state and cultural struggle.* Albany: State University of New York Press.

Gordon, B. (1995). The fringe dwellers: African American women scholars in the postmodern era. In B. Kanpol & P. McLaren (Eds.), *Critical multiculturalism: Uncommon voices in a common struggle* (pp. 59-88). Westport, CT: Bergin & Garvey.

hooks, b. (1994). *Teaching to transgress.* New York: Routledge.

Kanpol, B. (1991, September/October). The principal's voice. *The Clearing House,* pp. 19-22.

Kanpol, B. (1994). *Critical pedagogy: An introduction.* Westport, CT: Bergin & Garvey.

Lather, P. (1991). *Getting smart: Feminist research and pedagogy with/in the postmodern.* New York: Routledge.

Lewellen, J. (1990, March). Effective leadership development. *NASSP,* pp. 6-12.

Lyons, N. (1983). Two perspectives: On self, relationships and morality. *Harvard Educational Review, 53*(2), 125-143.

McLaren, P. (1994). *Life in schools.* New York: Longman.

Noddings, N. (1992). *The challenge to care in schools.* New York: Teachers College Press.

Peterson, K.D. (1985). *Making sense of principal's work.* (ERIC Reproduction ED 208 557).

Popkewitz, T. (1987). *Ideology and social formation in teacher education.* New York: Falmer Press.

Snyder, K., & Johnson, W. (1985). Restraining principals for productive management. *Educational Research Quarterly, 3,* 19-27.

Strober, H., & Tyack, D. (1980). Why do women teach and men manage? A report on research in schools. *Signs: Journal of Women in Culture and Society, 5*(31), 495-503.

Tyack, D., & Hansot, E. (1988). Silence and policy talk: Historical puzzles about gender and education. *Educational Researcher, 17*(3), 33-41.

Welch, S. (1985). *Communities of resistance and solidarity: A feminist theology of creation.* New York: Orbis Books.

6

A CRITICAL PEDAGOGY FOR PRINCIPALS: NECESSARY CONDITIONS FOR MORAL LEADERSHIP

(WITH FRED YEO AND SUZANNE SOOHOO)

One of the central problems facing teachers who are active critical pedagogists is their constant struggle with institutional and structural constraints to complete their work, such as mandated curriculum and/or little power or control over their time and the decisions they make (Kanpol, 1994). Such was what I faced as a teacher in public schools. Teachers in my graduate foundations classes, for instance, are at first shocked with this realization and then bitterly complain that they have been and continue to be deskilled. Perhaps this may motivate them to some form of social action. Our undergraduate students are always struggling with "how to do" critical pedagogy. They perceive critical pedagogy as a problematic subversive activity. Simply put, they believe their job would be at stake if they undertook critical pedagogy as a philosophical vision. In most cases, this is also true of current teachers.

There has been sparse literature directed to principals regarding the role they may play in challenging forms of oppression, alienation, and subordination. When we do have some administrators in my graduate foundations courses, we are often met with disdain and/or a numbing coldness, as if critical pedagogy is cancerous! With that pessimism in mind, this chapter optimistically moves ahead by first revisiting and elaborating on critical pedagogy as a concept and then connecting it to the principal's role and its more practical use. A distinction between traditional and "critical" problem-solving strategies are discussed as exemplars for school restructuring via critical pedagogy. Hopefully, for administrators who read this book, but particularly this chapter, open eyes and hearts will prevail.

REVISITING THE CONCEPT OF CRITICAL PEDAGOGY

We have learned that critical pedagogy is an approach to education that attempts to answer the question: What are schools for? Who do schools serve? What are the multiple functions of schools? Principals need to periodically ask themselves what is the purpose of schooling in general, and their school in particular. One thing is certain; critical pedagogy's approach to education is both humanistic and liberatory, with the intent of guiding school clientele (students, staff and parents) into becoming an empathetic community that engages in education for a participatory democratic society; one that embraces the notion that participation by all groups is and should always be legitimate.

It is clear that if principals want to be both progressive and *critical* change agents, they will have to alter the multiple realities that occur within an institutional context—in particular, those realities that alienate and subordinate school clientele, such as the students and professional staff, etc. Such realities may include stereotyping, race, class and gender bias, as well as situations in which institutional concerns are placed ahead of human interests and needs. To be *critical* for a principal means to recognize that the tensions inherent in an institution such as a school are really political and relate directly to social and cultural conflicts revolving around such issues as language and authority, as well as other dominant oppressive values, much of which have already been discussed in prior chapters. Perhaps that is why multiculturalism is such a big issue in schools today, with each group and/or school district carving out its own definition and use, with all groups politicizing what they see to be legitimate multicultural knowledge.

As a pedagogist as well, the principal can and must understand that knowledge and identities are produced within and among different sets of social relations in the school setting. Distinct from teaching, which can be likened to strategies and techniques used in order to meet predefined, given objectives, *pedagogy* certainly connotes a value-laden practice that is simultaneously *political* and *practical*. It is political in that it questions what constitutes appropriate or correct knowledge, skills, values, and attitudes (cultural capital), and what involves reflection, informed choices, and decisions socially mediated by personal and/or institutional experiences. It is practical in that it acknowledges what the political determines or is emphasized in and out of the classroom. In other words, the practical is bound by the political. This *critical* and *pedagogical* implication can and should be understood by the principal if they are to be prime motivators in school reform that goes beyond the mere social efficiency market logic discussed throughout this text thus far.

Although I have at some juncture in this book visited some of the underlying concepts within critical pedagogy (voice, other, and similarities within differences, for instance), perhaps a reminder and extension of these concepts is in order as we connect critical pedagogy to principals and school leadership in general. I view these concepts as "practically" significant for a principal desiring to effect real change in the conditions and relationships at his or her school.

Voice has at least three connected meanings: First, voice is meaningful dialogue. "Voice" depicts ways students, teachers, vice principals, and principals make or create meaning out of their cultural history and social experiences in the context of open and shared dialogue. Second, "voice" can be an internalized, private discourse that is shaped by the symbols, stories, narratives, and social practices of the culture in which it has been formulated. Such a voice is used by school clientele to interpret and make sense of personal experience. Third, a more abstract depiction of "voice" is defined by school practices and relationships of power. In this way, individual voice is determined by its owners' cultural history, prior experiences, and, in particular, social standing—status, expected role, and norms that accompany that role.

Put more practically, to comprehend voice in all three senses is simultaneously: (a) to understand how cultural capital/symbols, such as dress, language, history, stereotype, race and gender, formulate a lived school culture that includes all of its clientele and is often antagonistic to institutional concerns that deskill an individual; (b) to discern how these symbols shape and construe the hierarchical power relationships (between various relationships in schools such as teachers and administrators and teachers and students, etc.) within schools; and (c) to ascertain for oneself the contradictory messages that schools transmit to their clientele. For instance, a principal might question: Is my school promoting equal opportunity, or is it reaffirming that the existence of real equality is highly questionable? Does the curriculum restrict students to mediocrity, or does it open the way to vital, meaningful learning? Are we basing what Purpel (1989) defines as student worth on individualism—achievement, competition, and success—or on one's individuality—who we are, as we are, in our present cultural and social standing? Does my school truly promote and/or affirm student and teacher voice by listening to dialogue and trying to understand the cultural experiences behind what is being said, not just the words? Are we modeling real participatory democracy and citizenship or are we merely going through the motions? For example, are we promoting multiculturalism through International Food Week, or is multiculturalism a conscious effort to understand both our own and other cultures in relation to the social and cultural structures we exist in?

In short, the concept of voice that has been alluded to earlier in this book now involves becoming both aware and critical of the assumptions underlying one's personal voice, the voice of others, with the intent to engender authentic dialogue that engages all individuals and groups at the school (McLaren, 1994). That is, if I as a principal truly want to transform my school in a "critical" fashion, then I must engage in dialogue in which I test and understand my own personal history, as well as encourage others to do the same.

Intimately connected to voice is the concept of "other," already alluded to earlier. The "other" can be used interchangeably— referring to marginalized peoples in general, or the incorporation of the attitudes and values of a community. To empathize with these forms of the "other" is to transcend one's own view of what counts as *correct* culture, and instead, both understand, incorporate, and change oneself within other cultures that make up the school. To empathize and share meanings with the other can become a tool for principals to be used in order to better understand school clientele. The concept of "other" connects to that of "voice" through reflective dialogue, in which we try to empathize with the experiences that shape others at the same time that we reflect on our own attitudes, values, beliefs, and history. This is contrary to correct practices where we make assumptions for and about others.

To understand the "other" is also part of a critical pedagogic framework that has already been termed in this book, and elsewhere in some of my prior work (Kanpol, 1994), as "similarities within differences." How do principals empathize with the "other" when their experiences are, for the most part, different than the rest of the school personnel? Through the concept of *"similarities within differences,"* principals would be better able to understand the "other," and to lay the grounds for schools that nurture citizenship, empathy and democracy.

One can or should move from the personal to the public when talking about experiences that bring about "similarities within differences." It was argued earlier that none of our experiences necessarily equal that of every minority, yet at the base of all our differences lie the similarities of alienation and pain, albeit in different forms. Thus, we can begin to empathize with minorities, as groups and individuals, even though we may never have met them all. We can identify with anyone who has felt alienation because of being different. Even though our experiences are *different*, the *similarities* of oppression are felt by all of us in some particular fashion.

To be specific, how then does a principal understand and empathize with his or her staff and/or students? Principals should reflect first on their own "voice": Have their experiences been different from teachers and students? What makes their experiences similar? Have principals felt alienated before, left out of decision making, powerless, and so on? To translate those personal feelings into experiences ("voice") of the "other" (teachers, parents or students) and to empathize with their differences, while accepting the similarities, is to enter into a critical dialogue. To then apply what one has learned from this reflective dialogue with staff and students is to further an education for all and constitutes a solid beginning to a critical pedagogical platform.

WHY IS IT IMPORTANT FOR PRINCIPALS TO UNDERSTAND CRITICAL PEDAGOGY?

At some point in their management of a school, principals should reflect on the schools' moral purpose or mission, its philosophy. Is it to importantly, but *merely*, produce the work force of the future, such as what the social efficiency ideology has done so well? Is it to further a stratified society replete with illiteracy (Kozol, 1985, 1991), racism, sexism and unemployability? Or is it to imbue future citizens with a sense of community, critique, and democratic participation?

If the purpose is the latter, then the concepts of critical pedagogy can be used to facilitate this mission, implement future goals, and begin to create a school community in which tolerance, empathy, and intellectual or academic interest is the norm, not the exception.

To pursue such an emancipatory agenda, principals should consider the following "critical" points:

1. To understand the basic tenets of critical pedagogy is to further the principal's knowledge about the cultural history of both teachers and students. This necessarily leads to principals' making decisions about teachers and students informed by data—data that are *not* necessarily based on a particular act, such as a student being tagged as a "discipline" problem, or teachers not performing to standards. Reasoned responses by principals, which are based on understanding the context of these acts as bound within the framework of social and cultural experiences, are engendered by reference to teacher and student "voice," "other," and a principal's, teachers', and students' "similarity within differences."

2. Critical pedagogy allows the principal to better *empathize* with school clientele. Empathy would include understanding students, and teachers from their cultural and historical perspectives. These can give rise to a political morality allowing for shared decision making that reshapes a school into the democracy that we supposedly are and that encourages participation.

3. To understand critical pedagogy as outlined allows the principal to both understand and be more critical of his or her own school environment. This could result in site-based management, not merely paying lip service to handing teachers decision-making power. Rather, site-based management could involve the school on issues such as student and/or teacher conflict, student and/or teacher apathy, higher dropout rates and illiteracy levels, as well as drugs and gang-related issues. Part of resolving a problem is recognizing its derivation and empathizing with the culture and experiences (voice) of those caught up within it.

4. A critical pedagogist principal will necessarily become informed about a cultural link between students and the wider culture, including students' popular cultural relationships such as those found in music as well as in movies such as *Dirty Dancing, Pump Up the Volume, Pulp Fiction, Rambo, Lean on Me, Boyz in the Hood*, and *Forrest Gump*, as well as a host of others, some which have been mentioned earlier and others that are elaborated in on Chapter 8. Popular culture helps to define student voice. It is vital to remind principals that popular culture can be a trap for reinforcing hegemonic values, or it can be seen as a way to challenge some of those values. Thus, popular culture can or should be interrogated by principals for multiple meanings. This relates directly back to empathizing in order to transcend any personal assumptions of what constitutes the correct culture.

5. These issues necessarily link critical pedagogy to "cultural empowerment" (Kanpol, 1994). Cultural empowerment promotes an

understanding of the many cultural facets of teachers and students, such as race, class and gender issues, biases and beliefs, and so on. Principal cultural empowerment also includes allowing room for teacher input regarding school policy, particularly about a vision as to what constitutes a democratic community.

6. Critical pedagogy requires the principal to question the assumptions underlying the status quo and to encourage others to do the same in a dialogical manner.

7. If the principal wants to effectively lead an informed educated and critical community, one that thrives on change for equity, then principals must begin to role model the critical pedagogical qualities outlined earlier. To do so will help create a democratic citizenry in the school community. *Not* to pay attention to "voice," "other," or "similarities within differences" denies the school clientele the opportunity to create a more just and moral citizenship conditioned on understanding, cooperation, and democracy.

8. The critical pedagogical tenets described, if implemented by the principal, will allow him or her to better understand the diverse nature of cultures in the community. This naturally implies the respect and celebration of diversity or cultural difference as a form of dominant consciousness, which is a necessary condition to multiculturalism as described in Chapter 4.

9. Finally, critical pedagogy allows the principal to reflect on his/her or past experiences, history, biases, decisions, and relationships with a critical eye. This involves feeling empathy, understanding "voice," and being aware of the "other." Put bluntly, effective leadership becomes both a moral, critical, and cultural concern when critical pedagogy is taken seriously.

WHAT CAN BE DONE FOR PRINCIPALS TO IMPLEMENT CRITICAL PEDAGOGY?

1. Establish communication through "open, honest, and critical dialogue" with faculty and students. This in turn forms a web of understanding where all can be fully committed to mutually derived decisions instead of the traditional top-down decision style that depends solely on authority for communication (which is usually limited and less than enthusiastic).

2. Teacher staff meetings that revolve around the notion of *reflection* over voice, celebration of differences, and the bonding of "other" and "similarity within difference" *must* be created for

principals and teachers to both close the hierarchical gap and foster an intellectual environment. Instead of bureaucratic staff meetings, implement a sensitive environment that considers cultural concerns of both teachers, students, and administrators (vice principals, counselors, and principals).

3. One way to implement this environment is to move from a traditional/prescriptive (formula) management to a critical attitude, approach, or way of thinking for problem solving. What follows is an outline of what this may look like in schools for both teachers and students.

TYPICAL SCHOOL PROBLEM

Not meeting grade or testing expectations at the school.

Prescriptive (Traditional) Solution

Bring in learning specialists to prescribe solutions. Increase standardized tests and school work. Increase objective evaluations. Hold "planning" meetings where staff are told what they will do.

Critical Evaluation of the Problem

Interpret the child's experiences and learning as cultural and social. Assess experiences and "frames" of knowing. Learn how culture mediates student learning differences and skills.

TYPICAL SCHOOL PROBLEM

Testing that breeds anxiety and failure reflecting adversely student self-images.

Prescriptive (Traditional) Solution

Increased standardized testing; objectives and instruction geared to tests; administrative emphasis on higher statistical results.

Critical Evaluation of the Problem

Students would publically exhibit their work; alternative assessments such as portfolios of multiple domains as well as peer and self-assessment would hopefully eliminate test anxiety.

TYPICAL SCHOOL PROBLEMS

What to teach different ethnicities. How to infuse multicultural subjects to all students.

Prescriptive (Traditional) Solution

Ignore multiculturalism and English as a Second Language (ESL); one culture is best; students should learn facts about countries and peoples strictly for test recall.

Critical Evaluation of the Problem

Various meaning and multimeaning of facts would be explored. Center curriculum around children's historical and cultural experiences.

TYPICAL SCHOOL PROBLEM

Discipline and constant student resistance to rules and school regulations.

Prescriptive (Traditional) Solution

Autocratic rules and enforcement; rigid rule structure; discipline procedures based on "assertive discipline."

Critical Evaluation of the Problem

There would be communal rule making such as humanized rules, in which discipline would be based on understanding and not necessarily uniformity.

Noninvolved or resistant staff.

Prescriptive (Traditional) Solution

Decisions made top-down; no teacher or student input; motivate by threat, memos, innuendo, and distancing.

Critical Evaluation of the Problem

Participatory decision making would exist. Thus, solving of problems would be shared; meaning making would be socially constructed by all individuals. Thus, the principal does not assume an expertise mantle, and is open for an alternate expression of realities.

Noncreative lecture-based teaching; rigid structured classrooms.

Prescriptive (Traditional) Solution

Teacher and texts are sole knowledge sources in subject-based curriculum; strict adherence to official curriculum and standardized teacher evaluation.

Critical Evaluation of the Problem

Cooperative learning becomes a norm, allowing for expression of multiple alternatives in learning styles and output. Peer coaching in which student is an expert, in which "experience" becomes a knowledge resource or option for curriculum construction.

Inconsistent opposing goals; conflicting interests; unclear

responsibilities and confusing authority lines; some work being duplicated, and some undone.

Prescriptive (Traditional) Solution

Increasing paper definition and rules; reinforced hierarchies; nonnegotiable division of labor; rigid role definitions; contracts; adherence to objectives framework.

Critical Evaluation of the Problem

There will be increased time for teacher-teacher and teacher-student discussion. Arrival of tasks and roles will be dialogued about.

TYPICAL SCHOOL PROBLEM

Internal dissent.

Prescriptive (Traditional) Solution

Authority used as justification for control and rigidity; strict accountability; emphasis on predictability, control, and stability.

Critical Evaluation of the Problem

Students will be allowed to democratically question assumptions of their daily practices. The emphasis will be on flexibility, change, and mobility of multiple roles and the acknowledgment of students and teacher differences.

CONCLUSION

The above "typical school problems" discussion represents a schematic outline for moving schools from alienating and hegemonic experiences to more critical perspectives. To be sure, this outline is a *necessary* but *not sufficient* model to at least start this "critical" process. What has to be considered along with issues raised in the outline are critical pedagogical conceptual tools as they relate to everyday problems: "voice," "other," and "similarity within differences." Put another way: Just because one moves from traditional solutions to a more critical appraisal does not guarantee a "critical pedagogy!"

If schools are to seriously move in the progressive and democratic direction that John Dewey (1916) wrote about, such as a connection between child, curriculum, and society (Dewey, 1902a, 1902b), as well as building curriculum through experiences (Dewey, 1938), a "critical" platform is necessary to start this process. If democracy is a real objective for the school (not merely lip service), no other alternative exists but to challenge social efficiency models that technically dehumanize, alienate, and subordinate many students and teachers. Thus, solving typical school problems certainly becomes a task to reconstruct, by at first understanding the social construction of reality in all its aspects, such as race, class, and gender disparities (social efficiency), and then by altering this social construction to a new and liberating consciousness. Clearly, there is work to be done for the leaders of our schools, both by principals and teachers.

CLASSROOM ACTIVITY

1. In debate fashion, set up a traditional problem-solving side and a critical problem solving side. Discuss pros and cons of both positions.

QUESTIONS FOR DISCUSSION

1. Recollect your schooling experiences. How did the principal react to solving problems? How would you react as a teacher today, particularly regarding the issues discussed in this chapter?
2. What would a progressive administration look like to you?
3. Justify in writing or in discussion why you believe that there should be (a) an adherence to old-fashioned problem solving, (b) a mixture of both, or (c) a complete overhaul.
4. If you were principal of a school, how would you motivate your staff?
5. As a teacher, how do you expect to be kept motivated within the institution?

REFERENCES

Dewey, J. (1916). *Democracy and education.* New York: Free Press.

Dewey, J. (1902a). *The child and the curriculum.* Chicago: The University of Chicago Press.

Dewey, J. (1902b). *The school and society.* Chicago: The University of Chicago Press.

Dewey, J. (1938). *Education and experience.* New York: Collier Macmillan Canada.

Kanpol, B. (1994). *Critical pedagogy: An introduction.* Westport, CT: Bergin & Garvey.

Kozol, J. (1985). *Illiterate America.* New York: Plume.

Kozol, J. (1991). *Savage inequalities.* New York: Crown.

McLaren, P. (1994). *Life in schools.* New York: Longman.

Purpel, D. (1989). *The moral and spiritual crisis in education.* Westport, CT: Bergin & Garvey.

7

THE INNER-CITY SCHOOL AND CRITICAL PEDAGOGY: LOCATIONS OF POSSIBILITY AND DIFFERENCE

FRED YEO WITH COMMENTARY BY BARRY KANPOL

AUTHOR'S NOTE

Ever since I have been involved at least formally with critical pedagogy as an alternate form of education for our youth, both in the public schools and in the academe, I have been both disillusioned and shocked as to the sparse literature of critical pedagogy as it connects to the heart of the inner cities. The lack of literature sends a particular message. Is critical pedagogy to remain "safe" in middle-class schools? Are critical theorists really going to challenge oppression, alienation, and subordination—or to merely talk and write about it? With that in mind, this chapter, written by first a student, now a close colleague and friend of mine, is about urban education and some of its problematics as related to critical pedagogy. I am *not* equipped to speak for Fred, who, through personal experience, is brilliantly able to combine narrative, theory, and practice into a critical platform, particularly regarding inner-city schools (Barry Kanpol, February 1996).

Educational literature within the last decade has seen the steadily increasing incorporation of postmodern concerns, particularly as to difference, within the critical perspective. In particular, one major issue has been whether it is possible to bridge the gaps constructed of difference between various others to effect educational projects. Unfortunately, all too often these projects are confined to academia or generalized (simulated) classrooms and positioned to represent the null potentiality of crossing borders of diversity or difference to construct emancipatory connections within education. The discussion rarely reaches the level of teacher education or the practices of urban teachers. In the meantime, mainstream educational research and practice continues to ignore the implications of postmodern theorizing as well as the needs and special circumstances of urban schools.

The postmodern debate coincides with an American educational system that finds itself increasingly befuddled by questions of diversity and difference, in which the population of other-than-White is proliferating, and concerns over race, ethnicity, gender, and class are no longer muted. The institutions of American education represent a system that finds itself increasingly in a crisis of difference. We can no longer count on a harmonious society that simply embraces a dominant status quo (Giroux, 1992; Kanpol, 1992a).

Between the mainstream promotion of certain educational schemes (excellence, multiculturalism, effective teaching) and the postmodern concern for an often hypothetical marginalized Other, there is a certain irony. All too often ignored and/or denied by both, the diversity issues of the liberal educator and the postmodern contentions of difference and the margins all come together in the conditions and circumstances that constitute the inner-city school. Here the Other actually lives, sits, struggles, succeeds, and drops out, living within what McLaren (1991) has called the realities of nightmare metropolises and small towns that have lost their soul, where everyday life consists of living narratives of exile and victimage. The issues of difference and marginalization are far from being esoteric or mere jargon in an urban school classroom. They are the basis for understanding school sites constructed of frustration, fear, oppressive conditions, and educational paradigms that yield daily conflict and perennial failures of education and ultimately for the rest of society.

My intent in this chapter is to situate the postmodern debate over difference and identity within the context of an inner-city school, and to argue that dialogue and empathetic connections can occur between various Others for educational pursuits, albeit separated by cultural and racial borders, thereby posing an alternative to the current educational paradigms and practices inflicted on inner-city children. Simultaneously, I hope to contextualize the postmodern argument over dialogue within an experiential framework that suggests a possibility for critical education.

I attempt to convey some perception of borders (as generally defined within postmodern writings) inside the environment of an inner city school as experienced by the juxtaposition of its clientele and this writer—a White male teacher in a predominantly African-American school. Lastly, I suggest in general what I perceive to be potentials for critical changes within urban schools based on the creation of connections through a postmodern construed awareness of difference(s) and dialogue that can bridge culturally constructed gaps and thereby suggest potentialities for critical dialogic pedagogy in similar multicultural situations. Because much of urban education is structured by traditional educational theories of learning and responses to diversity, the contrasting postmodern arguments need some brief elucidation, which I do in the following section.

POSTMODERNISM, DIFFERENCE AND DIALOGUE

In general, the postmodern approach is to acknowledge a multiplicity of voices, positions, and identities without seeking their combination into a unified account (Burbules & Rice, 1991). It generally opposes modernism's universal logics, totalizing ethnocentricity in favor of communities constituted out of and by multitudinous frames of difference. Perhaps the major impact of postmodernism's concepts of difference and multiethnicity is in its attack on the modernist construct of universality that constitutes our dominant social and educational ideologies. It opposes the construct in which achievements and contributions of all other cultures are considered only as filtered through the lens of Eurocentric interpretation. This includes the ideologic presumption of the inherent superiority of the Euro-derived tradition and the devaluing of other traditions and cultural experiences (Rose, 1992; Sleeter & Grant, 1991). From these presumptions flows the educational practices that are all too familiar in inner-city schools that marginalize and/or silence community experience and knowledge. Left are only an educational preoccupation with cultural artifacts such as foods, dress, Europeanized hero figures, and truncated and ineffectual programs such as ESL, TESOL, and so on. (Darder, 1991; Nieto, 1992).

Postmodernism itself is undecided on difference and its implications, particularly in education. Burbules and Rice (1991) differentiate postmodernism into two camps on this issue. One camp is made up of the antimodernists, who contend that all differences are constructed as expressions of a subjective tension of identities that are totally incommensurable. This means that virtually no commonality or dialogue between groups and/or individuals is possible across the spaces of difference. This resulting immobility has been termed the "dilemma of difference." It constitutes a denial of the possibility of mutual understanding and a critique that any attempt to establish discourse across difference inevitably involves the imposition of dominant groups' values, beliefs, and modes of discourse on others (Burbules & Rice, 1991). Because that imposition is deemed wrongful, any prospect for change is stymied at the outset. The problem for the antimodernist is the immutability of difference: the perception that the spaces cannot be bridged, thereby reducing them to political impotence by virtue of their inability to theorize community. This argues in favor of a pluralism that regards different perspectives as incommensurable, a kind of anarchistic pluralism that celebrates uncertainty or lapses into a nihilistic retreat (McLaren, 1988).

The second camp argues the need to extend modernism's political project of "possibility" (Giroux, 1992). This construct is equally concerned with notions of difference and fracturing modernism's "universalism" and oppressive ideological and cultural regimes. But it does so by asserting a broadening of certain modernist tenets, such as dialogue, cooperation, pluralism, democracy, and community that incorporates differences in realities as ingredients of a democratic society (Kanpol, 1992b).

Thus, the issue for the postmodernists is how to construct connections across differences in order to create political projects for a more "democratic" society using education as an institutional base. Primarily the effort to theorize such bridges derives of construing personal experience so as to ground communities in resistance to modernism's marginalization, oppressions, and alienating Eurocentric ideologies. The intent is to interpret lived experiences so that one can identify commonalities between persons to effect solidarity of struggle, resulting in the reduction of social inequalities. This means that as critical educators, influenced by postmodern notions, we must dialogically act to find ways by which dissimilar people with distinct, sometimes divergent interests can come together and find a common ground. As Purpel and Shapiro (1995) suggest, this means to seek an agenda for education that reflects the particular struggle and aspirations of social groups and can reconcile their differences without denying or subordinating any of them.

In an explanation of these possibilities, a number of critical educators have posited how the concept of struggles and societal frictions can lead to commonalities of resistant struggle (Giroux, 1992; Kanpol, 1992a; McLaren, 1991). Giroux (1992) argues for what he terms a "border pedagogy" that can generate an ethos of solidarity in which we can share in the common struggle against domination and for freedom while preserving the specificity of difference. Kanpol (1992b) argues more specifically that the purpose is to empathetically integrate experience to derive a dialogue around difference, thereby effecting democratic educational projects by facilitating mutual understandings with and between people of difference, suggesting that there are also similarities of oppression, pain and feeling, albeit in miscellaneous forms. Kanpol (1992a, 1992b) argues that a pedagogy constructed within a notion of what he terms as "similarity within differences" can be derived from interrogating one's own experience(s) so as to empathize with the Other. He extends this argument to a presumption of empathetic connectivity by suggesting that through one's own life experiences one can identify with others who have felt alienation, suffering, and oppression, even though the respective circumstances differ. (Kanpol, 1992a, 1992b)

The problem with constructing bridges over the troubled waters of difference with experiential empathy, however, is the risk of presuming that alienating and/or marginalizing experiences are equivalent to the other; that the alienation of a middle-class White male equates to that of a sexually abused, inner-city Black female student. The problem lies in the meaning making or interpretations of our experiences. Because we interpret our experience through our incorporated value systems (or ideologies), and although we may sincerely desire to empathize and/or place our perspective from within that of another, we cannot help but overlay our understanding or empathy with the transparent norms of our own ideological perspectives (Lorde, 1990; McLaren, 1991).

The conundrum is, however, that if we assume that difference is incommensurable as do the antimodernists, we are left in a state of nullity and forced to accept the status quo. The educational postmodernists have, however, pointed to one potential bridge. Equivalent or not, we all share the *fact* of experience and the *need* for connectedness. So what is needed to have "similarity within difference" (Kanpol, 1992a) is to move beyond our own isolated experience to effect experience *with* the Other. That is, we may not be able to empathetically homogenize our differences of experience, but we may be able to create mutual experience by which we can begin to construct similar understandings. However, in order to do this, one must place the self where one becomes like an Other, to experience "Otherness" by seeking understandings partially constructed by work with different groups (Welch, 1990).

Experience as "other" is thus neither presumed nor proclaimed, but points of similarity can be gained with *engagement*. Giroux (1992) puts it well when he argues that although we can never speak inclusively as the Other, we can certainly work *with* diverse others to deepen both our own and their understanding of the traditions, histories, and knowledge that we each bring to the effort of creating mutual experience. To experience connection to the "Other" assumes at least minimal communication, that is, a dialogue across differences that leads to understanding and cooperation without alienating differences or imposing one's views on others (Burbules & Rice, 1991), and argues for circumstances in which different voices exist to the degree that they listen to the voices of Others. In searching for such a dialogue, and to locate and build community, perhaps the framework for a bridge across differences could begin by acknowledging experiential similarities. However, such acknowledgment is insufficient in and of itself. The initiation of empathetic community must move beyond disconnected self-experience to experiences of shared sensibilities that cross the boundaries of class, gender, race, and so on to create links that promote recognition of common commitments (hooks, 1990). This posits a move from the self-reflective to a proactive stance of seeking dialogue and being open to mutualities of experience, which can be used in reformulating educational practices.

One arena in dire need of critical reformation of its educational paradigms and practices is that of the inner city school. Increasingly minority children are being taught by middle-class White teachers (Grant & Millar, 1992) in school systems notorious for their social and educational failure (Kozol, 1991; Yeo, 1996). It would seem hard to argue that the barrios and ghettos of America's inner cities and their schools constitute anything less than the crowded location of marginalized, oppressed Others, and current educational schemes of assimilation and "sensitivity" training in these schools quite simply do not work (McCarthy, 1990; Sleeter & Grant, 1991; Yeo, 1992). It is my contention that the use of a postmodern perspective can foster better understanding of the marginalization of such students and communities so as to cross borders of difference through *engagement* and *dialogue*. Before describing and examining my own experience in both concepts within an inner-city school, the breadth of marginality and difference of the inner city and its schools needs some description, to which I now turn.

THE INNER-CITY SCHOOL: ITS CLASSROOMS AND PEOPLE

Simply put, the schools of America's urban centers are appalling: bankrupt districts, burgeoning populations of minorities, classrooms packed with children, drug and alcohol abuse, gang violence, and impoverished communities malignant with anger and frustration waiting for a spark (e.g., Los Angeles, April 30, 1992). One fourth of America's children live in poverty, and 80% of them are in the ghettos (Marable, 1992). The national dropout percentile for secondary schools is in the low 20s, but 65% to 75% are from urban schools (Fine, 1991; Hacker, 1992). In Chicago's ghetto schools, only 8% of a 9th-grade class will graduate reading at grade level; only 15% will even graduate (Fine, 1991). Many urban children come to school hungry, abused, and/or poorly clothed. They come to school from communities distinguished by empty buildings, boarded-up shops, proliferating liquor stores, random violence, pent-up anger and dehumanizing marginalization, poverty, and self-inflicted crime.

It is ironic and tragic, as Fine (1991) notes, that the children who begin their lives at the greatest risk attend the most traumatized schools and receive the most impoverished education. The overwhelming pattern of urban education is demarked by educational failure; among Black and Hispanic students in the five largest U.S. cities, the dropout rate exceeds 55%, and for Black males it approximates 75% nationwide (Comer & Haymes, 1990; Hacker, 1992; Nieto, 1992). African-American children are three times as likely as Whites to be placed in classes for the mentally retarded and subsequently drop out; Latino students drop out of school at a rate higher than any other group, in some areas 80% (Nieto, 1992).

Dominant social ideologies and traditional educational approaches construct particular school-site reasons for these statistics: the irrelevance of the school's practices to students' lives and experiences, the disconnection between the teachers and students, and the curricular approach administratively mandated and promulgated in the classroom. Urban schools offer sparse educations to children clearly based on race/ethnicity, social class, and community (Fine, 1991; Nieto, 1992). The curricular and pedagogical styles lend academic and social legitimacy to mainstream ideologies that deny the lived experiences of these youths (Fine, 1991; McCarthy, 1990; Yeo, 1996).

Urban education is all too often played out under the rubric of state-mandated curricular approaches labeled as basic skills programs. These are devised to ensure that urban students attain at least minimum literacy and computational skills, with the objective being to enter the work force (Yeo, 1996). The question never asked is: "What jobs?" This thereby underscores the disconnection between urban educational schema and students' existential realities. The major components of these skills programs are similar in most urban schools and are generally some combination of performance-based guidelines that require quantitative data to be gathered on student achievement; basic skill teaching kits that mandate certain workbooks, drillsheets, and texts; criterion-referenced pre- and posttests for use with specific curricular materials for specific subjects; and teacher evaluations that measure effectiveness on the basis of the test results. The prevalence of such programs and their being made mandatory by state bureaucracies results in ironies that typify urban teaching.

Many inner-city districts are too poor to purchase the materials, and the "official" version becomes quickly distorted even where materials are available. The packages are used to facilitate teacher standardization necessitated by faculty turnover (80% in some districts), side-track disruptive relations between teachers and students, and by principals who regularly promote "increases" in scores. Moreover, the program worsens relations with parents and students who view the schools as repressive, isolated, and racist (Carlson, 1989). The garnering of test results often becomes the rationale for administrative time and control over teachers, even when admittedly the results have been massaged and manipulated.

Perhaps in part because of the reliance on these basic skills programs, parents, students, and community leaders often perceive the urban school bureaucracy as insulated and not committed to the students. School administrators are perceived as repressive in their use of rigid tracking schemes, inadequate counselors who are anxiousness to push "at-risk" kids out (Fine, 1991), and isolated in the sense that school staffs are not involved in the community and are often arrogant to poor parents, especially where there is a racial or ethnic difference. The parents and students perceive an overuse of discipline and structured control coincident with schools' stated views that "ghetto kids" are unable to handle freedom or innovative classroom experiences. Typically, this is exacerbated by the feeling of being betrayed by Black teachers who should have been allies, and whose structure and control emphasis is felt as a non-Black distancing and rejection (Glasgow, 1980).

Additionally, there is the tension between middle-class teachers and administrators who do not live in the community and underclass parents and students who do. Urban minority parents see an inferior education perpetuated through devices they suspect are

White originated (e.g., biased tests, tracking, biased texts, biased counseling, etc.) and because they doubt that these schools understand Black children and their needs (Weiner, 1993). As a result, there is tremendous tension between parents and community on the one hand and school administrators on the other, with neither trusting or cooperating with the other (Yeo, 1996).

The "failure" of the basic skills program and of the students results from a complex struggle of differences—between the students on the one hand with their survival strategies and "street knowledge" versus the teachers who value and teach their middle-class, White cultural capital over that of the students:

> In the streets, knowledge was "felt," classroom knowledge was objectified and often sullied by an inflated rationalism. . . . In the street, students made use of bodily engagement, organic symbols and intuition. Students struggle daily to reconcile the disjunction between the lived meaning of the streets and the subject-centered approach to learning in the classroom. (McLaren, 1989)

Unfortunately, within educational circles, all this is rarely understood, as those with vested interests in traditional curriculum, administration, and pedagogy reject how a failure to perceive cultural differences and borders constructs educational failure in turn. Instead, the architects of assimilation and "feel good" sensitivity programs target the "victims" themselves within the rhetoric of "cultural deficiency" (Nieto, 1992; Sleeter & Grant, 1991).

Ultimately, students are prepared to pass tests and time, prepared for jobs that do not exist in the inner city, and are constantly battered with the dissonance of curriculum, pedagogy, and values that contradict what they know. For example, the emphasis in the "Basic Skills" program is on competition, individualism, and meritocracy that runs contrary to the value system of the Black community that emphasizes holism, group orientation, and self-effacement (Fordham, 1988; McLaren, 1989; Ogbu, 1988). The result is failure, massive dropouts, illiteracy, and school rhetoric attempting to justify the failure of promulgating a White, Euro-Western education on Hispanics, Asians, and African Americans by blaming its clientele. The actual failure of inner-city education is in the failure of society to change the social structures that regulate the lives of inner-city children. Rather than blaming the victims, we need to take into account the continuing American tolerance of the existence of grinding poverty, poorly trained teachers, self-serving administrators, the irrelevant curricula, and the reluctance of educational officials to meet the needs of inner-city students (Heath & McLaughlin, 1993; McLaren, 1989)

Given all the foregoing and multiplying by the continuing influx of diverse populations, the maintenance of the current school schema would suggest that inner-city education will continue to spiral into a welter of irrelevance, diminished polities, and massive numbers of frustrated and disenchanted dropouts and their communities, unless an alternative approach to urban teaching is promulgated. In the next section, through a description of my own teaching experiences and of the school, I suggest how the incorporation of postmodern concepts of difference, dialogue, and engagement can alter stereotypic inner-city school failure when a product of the dominant, traditional, educational understandings and purposes is dropped into the whirlpool of difference, marginalization, and cultural boundaries that is an inner-city school.

EXPERIENCING PEDAGOGY IN AN INNER-CITY SCHOOL

Ignorant of both inner-city schools and the potentialities of critical postmodern pedagogy, armed with the instrumental methods of teacher education and the excitement of embarking on the experience of teaching my knowledge (value, and ideologic and cultural constructs were taken for granted) to avid learners, I approached a teaching assignment at Washington Middle School[1] located in a south Los Angles district. Escorted by the janitor, without a gradebook or class roster (or a welcome by the principal), openly gaping at the broken windows, the graffiti, and the ubiquitous trash, I clutched my lesson plans and entered the room. Filled with 44 students, all arguing and pushing, I was immediately and vividly conscious of my Whiteness—and their Blackness. The plans quickly became spurious, and techniques of classroom management were drowned in the sheer volume of fights, obscene language, and everyone's anger. As I walked the corridors, obscene and violent language assaulted my senses, and classes and instruction were an unmitigated disaster. Nothing in my experience, certainly not teacher education, had prepared me for the humiliation and frustration as the "White boy," as the Other.

As time progressed, although I did not know the term, I became inundated with the paperwork integral to the "Basic Skills" program. I struggled with pre- and posttests, futilely demanding attention, no cheating, and "please stop talking!" I found other

---

[1]The names of schools and personnel are fictitious.

classrooms were structured with rows of desks, worksheets, and a plethora of packaged tests in which teachers routinely yelled at students to "shut the hell up" and pushed them from the room for trivial excuses. I listened to the administration's exhortations to work hard, follow directions, be on time, stay to the task, so as to graduate and get a job. I learned from students that there were no jobs, except on the street. I heard staff rail against the gangs, and the students describe how joining meant survival in the "hood." I talked at first about oceans, geology, and space, but began to listen to narratives about lives of abuse, hunger, and violence, knowing the world only as a few square blocks of squalid streets. I wondered why they refused to stop talking to each other during tests, until I realized they walked, talked, and lived in a group-cooperative world. I learned gang signs and how to speak "street"; they learned about "White folk." I wondered how they could have so many brothers, sisters, and cousins, until coming to an understanding that they lived within broad family-like connections in which there exists a sense of collective social identity, or what Signithia Fordham (1988) terms a fictive kinship system.

A significant amount of administrator and teacher time was configured by a continuing conflict over what constitutes the school's dominant rhetoric. Superficially, the official language of the school (used almost entirely by teachers and staff) was framed by a White, middle-class language (both syntactically and in content) versus the often obscene, oppositional "street" talk of the students. However, through dialogue and listening unassumptively, I came to perceive that the contentiousness was polyphonic and multivoiced; what was observed was that most of the issues surrounding school-site rhetoric has little to do with pedagogy or instructional efficiency. Rather, most of the issues were political issues, with serious social and cultural consequences (Williams, 1991). What has potential for critical reform in inner-city schools, perhaps, is that the staff were relatively unsuccessful in its efforts at cultural value imposition, except for those students who were struggling to educationally and culturally conform in a form of "racelessness"[2] to the social and cultural values implicit in the staff's rhetoric.

---

[2]"Racelessness" as a construct for a portion of minority school children is conceptualized by Signithia Fordham (1988) and frames the conflicted attempts of certain "achievers" to assume the dominant values (educationally and culturally) espoused by the school staff versus the often pejorative efforts of their peers to undercut their achievement in favor of the community (or "street") culture. Fordham explains well the often irregular grades of achievement-oriented minority students, which was often seen, and rarely understood, at this author's school.

Three years later I was fully enmeshed in the school and in the lives of students and families. Classes swollen beyond 50 by the administration or by "floaters" ejected from other classrooms, cornered me constantly for advice on school, studies, fights, sex, AIDs, race, and the myriad agonistics of my students' lives. I was asked to break in new teachers of different ethnicities, including Blacks, "cause you know how it is here"; my own consciousness was caught up and changed by language, culture, dialogue, and community and empathetic connections.

The change came about because of my profound realization that the educational practices and cultural capital promulgated by the school staff, texts, and official policies were inconsistent with the knowledge, culture, and experience of these children and their community. Struck by the irony of the distance between the language of the staff and that of the students, it became obvious that some new pedagogical dynamic was needed to contravene the former. The conflict for control over knowledge and voice between staff and students are illustrated by two vignettes; it should be understood they were not isolated events, but common occurrences, and they exemplify the dichotomy between the two groups:

(1)   Overheard in an assembly in which the principal spent the P.E. dept's entire budget for a speaker to tell students to study hard, follow the rules, be quiet, and obey teachers to get A's and a "Cadillac job"; students could be heard saying "That man's fulla boosheet, dere ain't no fuckin jobs fo niggers, man!" "Shit man, my homie's gettin me a Cad for heppin ta move da blow [crack]!" "My brother grageated from the "Two" (a local high school) wid a four-o and he cain't get no job!" These comments (along with many others) were expressed by "A" students!

(2)   One afternoon after a day of fights, "misbehavior," and three teachers fleeing to quit due to classroom conditions, the principal announced to the school over the P.A. that students should be good and obey the school codes: "If you want to be free, you have to obey our rules!" He never realized the contradiction. The students responded with laughter and disdain: "Man, Mr. Yeo, that ole bitch, she be all fucked up—she don't know what she say, do she!" I could only agree, and we spent the rest of the science class period talking about rules: who makes them and why.

In a similar school, Christine Sleeter interviewed teachers who "described their purposes as teaching basic skills and academic knowledge, largely at a remedial level, and preparing students for useful lives outside of school. . . . They saw their purpose as transmitting to students a body of knowledge and skills that would be practical. . . . They explained the students' low achievement

primarily by citing *deficiencies in the students' home backgrounds."*
(Sleeter & Grant, 1991, p. 54; emphasis added)

In this conflict over the school's cultural politics, these
middle-class teachers, who lived in the suburbs and generally taught
with the best of intentions, rarely acknowledged that children in the
inner city bring different historical and cultural experiences and
knowledge to school, which was evidenced in diverse motivational
patterns, language, meanings, and skills (Boateng, 1990).

One of the dichotomies of the school is the teachers' use of
both cultural languages. Teachers would admonish, structure, and
control their classrooms, as well as transmit certain knowledge,
behavior, and values within the framework of the dominant official,
administrative rhetoric (White, middle class). Concomitantly in
private discussions, in aside comments in class and within the "safe"
confines of the lounge, language and voice would change
dramatically. The former was often the voice of authority, power, and
control, whereas the latter was that of the community: alienated and
oppressed (expressed both as Black and teacher). The second voice
constructed most teacher "private" talk (away from administrators
and students) and was as direct, obscene, and angry as that of the
students. In staff meetings, teachers mixed both voices; that of the
dominant culture when addressing the principal or the group, and
that of the minority culture when speaking privately. Noticeably, the
administration was never observed to shift voice.

In a postmodern sense, these teachers moved within
multiphonic positions, articulating their language and shifting
cultural constructs depending on the respective site. Given the
proximity of teachers' and students' cultural voices, it suggests that
the voice connected to each space resulted from perceptions,
individually and collectively, of their relative power in a particular
set of relations. These dichotomies also evidence the existence of and
unconscious crossing of borders in the postmodern sense. Thus, and
not unexpectedly, as I began to truly dialogue with students, I
discovered that for them school literally had little meaning or
relevance to their lives. Increasingly, much of our class time was
devoted to stories of their lives and mine (of which they were
fascinated; some had never seen a White person, except on
television). Science was learned outside in the grass or exploding on
the desk or smelling up the ventilation system.

Insofar as what they were tasked with in other classes, I
discovered that in general the students dismissed most school
knowledge, seeing it as useless, except within the narrow confines of
the school. Schoolwork was less a step to a larger world and more

perceived as a series of meaningless tasks to perform. We worked together to create projects and subvert administrative rhetoric while discovering science, math, and African-American history. Lesson plans were often week-long tangents driven by student interests, experiences, and knowledge. Through the use of chemistry and physics to create practical jokes or plays, we created a mutuality of experience in laughter, frustration, and commonality. Although we could never completely understand each other or share past experiences in essence we crossed borders by synthesizing present experiences and anticipating future ones together.

Although convinced by students' tears and hugs on every graduation day that we had indeed dialogued across our mutual differences and connected intersubjectively, continuing communication with students (many struggling with the dissonance between their urban high school and the shared experiences in our class) suggests that it is both possible and problematic to talk across boundaries. In the next section, I connect these experiences with the postmodern concerns for difference and dialogue, and suggest (insofar as to similar schools) how teachers might "work with" the Other themselves to create "similarities within differences" through bridges of mutual experience.

THE PRACTICE OF "HERE I AM!"

Without being facetious, some postmodernists have tended to polarize the question of difference and dialogue into Black and White; difference is commensurable or it is not; dialogue can exist synchratically or is impossible. Contemporaneously it is argued that difference is immutable and/or that its boundaries can be intersubjectively negotiated through empathetic experience of self. In this section, I suggest that dialogue across differences is eminently possible, but occurs in a spectrum of lived experiences across a broad range of shifting positions that constitute ephemeral connectivities. Furthermore, in order to effect "border crossings" and experience "similarities within difference," we need to extend from self-experience to experience life as an "Other" and with the "Other."

One of the problematics within the postmodern discourse is the lack of attention to urban schools; all too often theorizing of difference and "border crossings" is of generalized Others, students, and schools. Urban schools are matrixed by the very difference, marginality, and value and cultural conflicts that critical theorists attempt to deal with.

Many teachers fail here (professionally and educationally) because of an inability to project or perceive across the inherent differences (we used to call it "culture shock"); yet others do well. Both my experience and that of these others suggests that it is possible to bridge the gaps of difference and connect with these students and staff regardless of starting points of culture and ethnicity, thereby reducing student-school dissonance and classroom resistance.

Interpretatively, the milieu of the urban school site exemplifies both postmodern camps; the majority of teachers presuming complete incommensurability, struggling to move students across the spaces or retreating into survival, and there are a few who recognize that it is the curricular and pedagogical that is incommensurable, moving to reach across the gaps and enter into dialogue. The issue, then, seems to crystallize around whether dialogue is possible. Educationally, we have little choice; if dialogue is impossible for one reason or another, then education is left to the purveyors of mainstream technocratic knowledge, Western values, and ethnocentricity. In the inner city, at least, we know this represents rank failure. Mainstream educational paradigms are educationally, culturally, and morally bankrupt, and any argument that limits the striving for dialogue and mutualities of experience is equally bankrupt and immoral.

One stance educators, particularly in urban schools, can take is to accept the partial, to acknowledge that dialogue can also serve the purpose of creating partial understandings, if not agreement, across differences. As Burbules and Rice (1991) comment, no communication process is perfect; no intersubjective understanding is ever complete. It is in that partiality that mutuality can be initiated. In urban classrooms, where communication and connectivity is distorted and/or negated by relations of power and control, mainstream educational practices, and cultural borders, teachers must accept that dialogue is multidirectional, not linear, and that this derives from the understanding that voices must be heard to be spoken. Teachers must listen and interrogate both that which is said as well as their reactions to what is heard. We must accept that because we cannot, as the old saying goes, walk a mile in someone else's moccasins, so our understanding will always be imperfect and partial. We need to expect and accept that the experiences that underlay student voice will be problematic, and that one's own experiences can never completely equate with those of the students or the staff in an inner-city school. It is why an ethic of empathy, while still immersed in one's own experience, is fractured. In order to bridge the spaces of their individual and collective differences and to locate similarities, a teacher in this environment needs to interrogate that which structures his or her own experience, the pedagogy, and curriculum and to avoid taking for granted assumptions of student identity.

To participate with students in the processing of a dialogic pedagogy across differences, a teacher should not presume a similarity of any difference, but allow articulation without rephrasing into instrumental discussion, nor presume a limitation on the varieties of difference and representations. As part of the process of developing a pedagogy of mutuality, dialogue, and difference, teachers need to deal with the specificity and organization of differences that constitute any course, class, or curriculum so as to make problematic not only the stories that give meaning to the lives of their students, but also the ethical and political lineaments that inform their students' subjectivities and identities (Giroux, 1988, 1992).

Ultimately, if an educator desires to be effective in the critical sense within the confines of an urban classroom, to locate the spaces of differences and similarities therein, and encourage a dialogic pedagogy to bridge intersubjectively both teacher and student differences, then I would suggest there are two levels at which this can be attained.

First, the teacher must become familiar with students' voices, conceptually and experientially. This means giving students the opportunity to speak, to locate themselves in their community and its history, and to become co-equals in the construction of that mutual experience and commonality.

Second, in order to be able to initiate any form of bridging of differences, building of similarities, and constructing of dialogue (partial or otherwise), it is a matter of the affective, not the cognitive. In another sense, it is a matter of prioritizing the ethical, not the epistemic. McLaren (1991) describes, in part, a postmodern ethical paradigm that I believe has profound implications for teaching in inner city schools. He suggests that when an other—a student, teacher, or parent—in need makes the demand—"Where are you?"— we must respond before we ask the traditional first question in education—"Who are you?" That is to suggest that we become responsible for that other before we know their credentials. We should not ask for identity papers, if at all, but certainly not before we reply, first and foremost, *"Here I am."* Students need to know we are there for them before we ask them to identify themselves (McLaren, 1992).

I would add that all too often we structure students' identities (what we have heard from other teachers, the students' dress, looks or language, past grades or test results, etc.) before they can represent themselves. When students approach, their identity should be theirs, not what we as teachers impose or assume. In my own experience in an inner-city school, it was the teachers who replied—"Here I Am!"—who crossed borders, found the similarities, and connected to students. They did this not by structuring a dialogue, but by stepping away from the comfort of authority, power, and control, allowing students to approach within a relationship in which dialogue is simply possible, not mandatory.

CONCLUSION

I have attempted in this chapter to sketch critical concepts within the conditions of urban education, specifically in that place where teachers meet student, where we meet the Other, where we can become as the Other. Too many teachers fear or fail the inner-city school because, it seems to me, they do not comprehend the potentialities for connections between themselves and the students. Within the boundaries of the postmodern debate over difference and dialogue are the possibilities for bridges or crossings past those differences. In part it requires an understanding of the nature and conditions of education as it is played out in the inner city. It requires an understanding of what it means to be marginalized beyond one's own experience, and that one's experiences do not automatically equate with that of another. A sensitivity to experience and how cultures and communities frame those differences and the process of dialogue itself provides a basis for this understanding.

The basing of that dialogue, of effecting "border crossings," cannot and will not occur without moving away from one's own experience as a totalizing benchmark. It takes the humility of denigrating one's experience for the sake of that of the Other, of attempting without prior assumptions the learning of the conditions of language, culture, and voice. It takes the realization that the knowledge that one brings to the classroom is undoubtedly meaningless to these kids whose lives are constructed of and by joblessness, violence, and the streets. To teach in the inner city is on the one hand to understand the dialectics of language, voice, cultural knowledge, and values, and, on the other, to comprehend that the curriculum and pedagogy espoused by those in authority is incommensurate with the realities of students' lives, and that the school and your experience will be constructed and delineated by the conflict of rhetoric for control of the schools' "voice." It is to understand that "getting to know the kids" is problematic and is possible only by moving away from the structure one brings to the teaching to creating new and mutual structures of experience with those same children.

Finally, to teach, particularly within the inner city, is to avoid the official paradigm of constructing students' identities, of forcing the mold, and to place oneself "at risk" by repetitively representing and demonstrating without antecedents or conditions—"HERE I AM!"

Many students approach me and comment on how they think that critical pedagogy is a risky business. Their comments are justified in that they relate to their personal and professional concerns. I would argue that critical pedagogy in school's other than that which Fred describes (e.g., suburban) although somewhat threatening in that it challenges dominant and oppressive structures, is a different type of pedagogy that Fred has written about. Critical pedagogy as Fred describes in this chapter is "risky," in that more than we care to imagine our moral fabric is at stake: Is society really like this? How am I a part of this problem? To conduct critical pedagogy in the inner city is at once to question your own "Here I am," while situating and intertwining this with the "Here I am of 'others'." Indeed, the struggle goes on. Critical theorists such as Fred should be well received. Their work is truly the "gut of life." I end this "sermon" with a snippet of a phone call with Fred two weeks into his teaching at Washington middle school. I was then his professor:

Barry: So how goes it Fred?
Fred: I've lost 14 pounds in two weeks. I don't know if I
             can take it any longer.

CLASSROOM ACTIVITIES

1. Each student is to complete a lesson plan and/or unit plan in his or her content area keeping "urban" schooling in mind. Connect the lesson plan to "voice," "similarity within difference," and "other."
2. In a student teaching experience and/or a student's own personal questionnaire through a class activity (perhaps a research assignment), conduct one or more questionnaires on narratives of others (public school teachers, students, or administrators) who are ethnically different to you. Compare and contrast your narrative with the research you have completed.
3. Debate the issue of a standardized curriculum as related to cultural differences.

QUESTIONS FOR DISCUSSION

1. How do you believe you can create a climate in which similarities within differences can exist with your students in urban schools?
2. How would this connect to issues such as curriculum, grading, and your general expectations of students?
3. What does Fred mean by the practice of "Here I am?"
4. What does basic skills mean to you? Should it mean anything else to anyone of difference?
5. Is there a standardized language? Should there be one? Why/Why not?
6. If you had your choice between teaching in an inner-city school like Fred did or a suburban school, which one would you choose and why?
7. Do you think the postmodern, other-critical-theory arguments are helpful in alleviating practical problems in the inner city?

REFERENCES

Boateng, F. (1990). Combatting deculturalization of the African American child in the public school; A multicultural approach. In K. Lomotey (Ed.), *Going to school: The African American experience*. Albany: State University of New York Press.

Burbules, N. & Rice, S. (1991). Dialogue across differences: Continuing the conversation. *Harvard Educational Review, 61*(4), 393-416.

Carlson, D. (1989). Managing the urban school crisis: Recent trends in curricular reform. *Journal of Education, 171*, 3-22.

Comer, J., & Haymes, N. (1990). Helping Black children succeed: The significance of some social factors. In K. Lomotey (Ed.), *Going to school: The African American experience* (pp. 23-36). Albany: State University of New York Press.

Darder, A. (1991). *Culture and power in the classroom: A critical foundation for bicultural education*. Westport, CT: Bergin & Garvey.

Fine, M. (1991). *Framing drop-outs*. Albany: State University of New York Press.

Fordham, S. (1988). Racelessness as a factor in Black students' school success. *Harvard Educational Review, 58*(1), 69-94.

Giroux, H. (1988) Border pedagogy in the Age of postmodernism. *Journal of Education, 170*(3), 162-181.

Giroux, H. (1992). *Border crossings; Cultural workers and the politics of education*. New York: Routledge, Chapman & Hall.

Glasgow, D. (1980). *The Black underclass*. San Francisco: Jossey-Bass.

Grant, C., & Millar, S. (1992) Research and multicultural education: Barriers, needs and boundaries. In *Research and multicultural education: From the margins to the mainstream* (pp. 7-18). Bristol, PA: Falmer Press.

Hacker, A. (1992). *Two nations; Black and White, separate, hostile, unequal*. New York: Scribner's Sons/Macmillan.

Heath, S., & McLaughlin, M. (Eds.). (1993). *Identity & inner-city youth: Beyond ethnicity and gender*. New York: Teachers College Press.

hooks, b. (1990). *Yearning; race, gender and cultural politics*. Boston: South End Press.

Kanpol, B. (1992a). *Towards a theory and practice of teacher cultural politics: Continuing the postmodern debate*. Norwood, NJ: Ablex.

Kanpol, B. (1992b). Postmodernism in education revisited: Similarities within differences and the democratic imaginary. *Educational Theory, 42*(2), 217-229.

Kozol, J. (1991). *Savage inequalities; Children in America's schools.* New York: Crown.

Lorde, A. (1990). Age, race, class, and sex: Women defining difference. In R. Ferguson, M. Gever, T. Minh-ha, & C. West (Eds.), *Out there: Marginalization and contemporary cultures* (pp. 281-288). Cambridge, MA: MIT Press.

Marable, M. (1992). *The crisis of color and democracy.* Monroe, ME: Common Courage Press.

McCarthy, C. (1990). *Race and curriculum: Social inequality and the theories and politics of difference in contemporary research on schooling.* New York: Falmer Press.

McLaren, P. (1989). *Life in schools: An introduction to critical pedagogy in the foundations of education.* New York: Longman.

McLaren, P. (1991). Critical, pedagogy, multiculturalism, and the politics of risk and resistance: A reply to Kelly and Portelli. *Journal of Education, 173*(3), 29-59.

McLaren, P. (1991). Schooling the postmodern body: Critical pedagogy and the politics of enfleshment. In H.A. Giroux (Ed.), *Postmodernism, feminism, and cultural politics* (pp. 144-173). New York: State University of New York Press.

Nieto, S. (1992). *Affirming diversity: The sociopolitical context of multicultural education.* New York: Longman.

Ogbu, J. (1988). Classification, racial stratification and schooling. In. L. Weis (Ed.), *Race, class and schooling.* New York: State University of New York Press.

Purpel, D.E., & Shapiro, S. (1995). *Beyond liberation and excellence: Towards a new public discourse for education.* New York: Routledge.

Rose, W. (1992). The great pretenders; further reflections on White shamanism. In M.A. Jaimes (Ed.), *The state of Native America* (pp. 403-423). Boston: South End Press.

Sleeter, C., & Grant, C. (1991). Mapping terrains of power: Student cultural knowledge versus classroom knowledge. In C. Sleeter (Ed.), *Empowerment through multicultural education* (pp. 49-68). New York: State University of New York Press.

Weiner, L. (1993). *Preparing teachers for urban schools: Lessons from thirty years of school reform.* New York: Teachers College Press.

Welch, S. (1990). *A feminist ethic of risk.* Minneapolis, MN: Fortress Press.

Williams, S. (1991). Classroom use of African American language: Educational tool or social weapon?. In C. Sleeter (Ed.), *Empowerment through multicultural education.* New York: State University of New York Press.

Yeo, F. (1992). "The inner-city school: A conflict in rhetoric. *Critical Pedagogy Networker, 5*(3), 1-5.

Yeo, F. (1995). Conflicts of difference in an inner city school: Experiencing border crossings in the ghetto. In B. Kanpol & P. McLaren (Eds.), *Critical multiculturalism: Uncommon voices in a common struggle* (pp. 197-216) Westport, CT: Bergin & Garvey.

Yeo, F. (1996). *Inner city schools, multiculturalism and teacher education: The search for new connections.* New York: Garland.

PART III

EMERGING TRENDS
IN CRITICAL PEDAGOGY

8

TEACHING FOR A NEW PARADIGM: CRITICAL PEDAGOGY AND POPULAR CULTURE

> Critical public intellectuals must define themselves not merely as marginal figures, professionals, or academics acting alone, but as citizens whose collective knowledge and actions presuppose specific visions of public life, community, and moral accountability. Educational work in a variety of public spheres, including public and higher education, must self-consciously recall the tension between democratic imperatives of working educationally and politically to extend and deepen the possibilities of democratic public life. This is an eminently pedagogical task. (Giroux, 1995a, p. 5)

This quote from leading critical educational theorist, Henry Giroux is simply a plea for teachers (as is the case for this book) to be more than merely technicians or socially efficient messengers. Giroux argues time and again, no different than in the article from where this was excerpted, that the role of progressive educators is to be public intellectuals. Giroux (1995a) connects the notion that to be a public intellectual is a pedagogical and political task, involving the distribution of cultural capital. He comments: "Progressives need a more expansive notion of education and pedagogy as a form of cultural work that takes place across diverse sites of learning, including schools" (p. 5)."

These comments by Giroux (1995a) suggest that educators must not only move out of a social efficiency mindset, but even move from a simple classroom progressive view of teaching. As a public intellectual, Giroux takes on the dominant culture by deconstructing how radio talk shows, for instance, are exemplary of a neoconservative trend in America, and moves into the terrain of the culture and various meaning-making systems. He comments once more: "We need to find ways as cultural workers of using multiple approaches, styles, aesthetics, and forms of engagement to reach diverse audiences" (p. 5). Those teachers who are cultural workers and are committed to make their pedagogy more political must, Giroux argues, look beyond traditional means to move students as well as themselves into the terrain of the counterhegemonic.

Even if Giroux or Kanpol, or any other cultural worker, is in the business of critical pedagogy, the task of liberating a culture is momentous—let alone teacher education in particular. Frankly, I am rather tired of writing about the lack of vision that teacher education has in this country. The now well-documented "critical" literature about teacher education depicts a technocratic mindset, with little substantive concerns for the implementation of a means to combat disablement of imagination, mindless endorsement of standardization, and race, class and gender disparities. Criticalists argue that the less teachers need to be equipped with to cope with these issues is a critical disposition. As a response to this, Henry Giroux (1988) has long called for teachers to become transformative and public intellectuals, those who insert politics into all phases of pedagogy in order for a language of possibility to prevail.

Others in the education field, such as McLaren (1994), Kincheloe (1993), Yeo (1996), and myself (1994), as well as feminists (Britzman, 1991; Fine, 1988; hooks, 1994; Noddings, 1992; among others) have bombarded the literature with concepts, some of which were earlier discussed, such as "voice," "similarity within difference," "postformal thinking," "caring," and "compassion," and so on, in an effort to move the educational left out of the maze it finds itself in, who are also stuck within teacher education departments that are for the most part patriarchal and anti-democratic. As a result there has been incessant deconstruction over both modern and postmodern relationships within education, some of which have been highlighted in this book.

I am not going to belabor readers with even more of the same deconstruction, but keep in mind, increasingly I find myself posing the question: To what end has all this deconstruction around criticality in education taken us? Has it made us better public intellectuals? I do not want to sound too cynical and say that criticalists in education have taken us nowhere because theory always drives practice in some way. But it is no small argument to make when one thinks about what good this theory does given the decrepit and at times horrifying conditions that presently exist within our public educational system (Kozol, 1991; Weiner, 1993; Yeo, 1996).

For many critical educational theorists such as myself, constant negotiation of both teaching content and methods has always been problematic, particularly within positivistic and socially efficient mindset teacher education departments. Some critical theorists, for instance, have argued that Kuhn's (1970) vision of a paradigm shift can and should be applied to social sciences such as the education fields. To me, this shift is more than merely a move from say quantitative to qualitative forms of scientific reasoning. A paradigm shift within a community of researchers who accept "qualitative frameworks" is needed in our classrooms as part of a pedagogical movement to undercut the hegemonically constructed technocratic and positivistic mindsets that have historically flooded the teacher education market. With that in mind, this chapter deals with a particular part of this paradigmatic shift, a form of narrative, one that is connected intimately to the qualitative terrain within *popular culture*. Clearly, to be a public intellectual on the one hand is to take popular culture seriously, simply, as a form of political maneuverings, sets of values and beliefs, and so on.

I deal with this movement here on three levels. First, I quickly look at Henry Giroux's (1994) recent work on popular culture, Disturbing Pleasures, as promulgating and supporting this paradigmatic shift. Second, I connect some of Giroux's work to my personal teaching pedagogy. Third, as part of my conclusions I argue theoretically for ongoing critical pedagogical and practical strategies to further the insights popular culture offers us as part of the emerging "qualitative" paradigm.

DISTURBING PLEASURES

For many years now, Henry Giroux has pioneered the educational left to new and emerging understandings of the relationship of education to the culture milieu. His recent work on popular culture has emerged at a time when the educational left is in dire need of alternative visions to the stultifying deconstructive theoretical garbs it has historically clothed itself in. As an emerging teaching paradigm, Giroux analyzes the use of cultural configurations such as

Benetton Advertising and Disney filmmaking as immoral opportunistic enterprises guided by pure capitalistic gain. Related directly to education, Giroux clearly shows readers how Whittle Communications and their Channel One promotion, as well as the Edison Project, carry ideological overtones that are simply mind boggling. Moreover, Giroux argues that film, as well as photography, has been structured in such hidden, implicit, and manipulative ways as to form what he calls a "politics of identity" that crudely reproduces race, class, and gender disparities.

Put another way, what Giroux has effectively done in the first five chapters of his book is to disentangle how various areas of popular culture have emerged within a "politics of innocence" that masks the "nightmare realities" of social structures of oppression, subordination, and alienation. For instance, in a recent article by Giroux (1995b), he outlines how the world of Disney portrays innocence, imagination, fantasy, amusement, fun, and joy, but is concurrently masked by far more than this. He is worth quoting at length here:

> Needless to say, the significance of animated films operates on many registers, but one of the most persuasive is the role they play as the new "teaching machines." I soon found that my children, and I suspect for many others, these films inspire at least as much cultural authority and legitimacy for teaching specific roles, values, and ideals than more traditional sites of learning such as public schools, religious institutions, and the family. Disney films combine an ideology of enchantment and aura of innocence in narrating stories that help children understand who they are, what societies are about, and what it means to construct a world of play and fantasy in an adult environment. The commanding legitimacy and cultural authority of such films stems, in part, from their unique form of representation, but such authority is also produced and secured within the predominance of a broadening media apparatus equipped with dazzling technology, sound effects, and imagery packaged as entertainment, spin-off commercial products, and "huggable" stories. (pp. 24, 25)

What Giroux is implying and goes on to argue both in *Disturbing Pleasures* and this particular article is that Disney becomes a form of hegemony, in which entertainment masks capitalistic gain, and various forms of oppression, such as race, class, and gender disparities as seen in such Disney productions as *The Little Mermaid* (1989), *Beauty and the Beast* (1991), *Aladdin* (1992), and *The Lion King* (1994). Basically, Giroux's message is that critical pedagogists and other progressive educators can and should use popular culture as a basis for a pedagogy to help students both understand and alter the present despairing cultural conditions of our times so that ultimately they can question their identity as bordering between being socially constructed as well as constrained!

My students enjoy reading this form of critical theory. In the past, they have often complained of the complexities of language and ideas that criticalists write about. The point is *not* to be overly critical of these theorists (I am one of them), but to simply say that Giroux has found a very sophisticated method in which to incorporate the difficult ideas of his previous years of writing into a new medium—one that speaks directly to the everyday world of teachers and their students—popular culture. Put another way, by using popular culture as a text, Giroux is able, with my students at least, to critically interrogate the "affective investments" (Grossberg, 1992), hegemonically constructed, that they make into popular culture. By reading *Disturbing Pleasures*, my students are left gasping at the incredible power of popular culture, the "con job" it has done on the public and the realities implicated for themselves as well as their public school students. Giroux thus moves between the complexity of theory and that of everyday speaking to and with a popular audience—in this case, teachers. Both complexities, I argue, are interrelated within his work, in such a way so as not to distance readers, but to draw them closer to the theoretical work that drives the popular within the everyday world of multiple popular discourses. *A victory for critical theorists!*

The second part of *Disturbing Pleasures* takes on a related but somewhat different tone from the first section's five chapters. Perhaps the most compelling theoretical chapter of this book is Chapter Six's, "The Turn Towards Theory." A careful read of this chapter suggests that critical pedagogy must take on the theoretical assumptions invested in popular culture as a way to "reorder the curriculum to allow the force and affective energy of other kinds of "texts," including films, videos, and music . . . to break down student resistance, promote collaborative engagement" and perhaps, most importantly, to "destabilize fixed notions of what constitutes valuable social knowledge" (p. 121). I emphasize that although my students find this chapter to be "more of the same old Giroux," this is not an argument for it being an unnecessary chapter in this particular book. As Giroux states up front in this chapter: "Theory has never fared well in educational circles." To omit this difficult chapter is to deny Giroux the space to intrude on these basic educational assumptions and practices.

Chapter 7 depicts Giroux doing what he hasn't done in previous years; that is, connecting the first six chapters to his personal teaching pedagogy as part of a politics that struggles over "meaning, language and textuality" (p. 129). The terrain of the popular is investigated in three writing projects that Giroux sets up as part of what he describes as "border writing," thus allowing students the space to investigate the politics of identity among different reading texts, cooperatively completed and disseminated among students in written and spoken format. The writing practices act as a pedagogical tool in which self-reflection and cultural recovery are addressed within the popular. I *humbly* admit that this chapter taught me a lot about "recovering" the possibilities of incorporating some of Giroux's methods so intimately connected to the previous chapter and so carefully crafted around the popular cultural concerns of the first section of the book.

In conclusion, Giroux argues that for critical pedagogy to not be another authoritarian text, the left must become more of what he describes as "border intellectuals," coming "home" to the sites of resistance and opposition that "enables conditions of self and social formation" (p. 143). Interestingly, I would suggest that Giroux's view of "home" would include the unsettling experience of deconstructing popular culture as it relates to the hegemonically constructed alienation, subordination, and oppression of ours and others' lives.

This book holds together well. Again, Giroux has brilliantly theorized, but this time spaces have been opened for the public to read his work as a text that speaks "to and with" his audience, rather than what many critical theorists do, which is to speak "at" their audience. In so doing, Giroux has both instigated and supported a paradigmatic shift in the way critical pedagogists can use their classroom. The classroom is not just four walls; in short, it becomes a social text. Classroom projects around popular cultural texts become the social critic. Students mediate between their particular identity formation and the varying formations brought about through popular culture. Dialogue mediates an ongoing endeavor to uncover hegemonically constructed symbols, metaphors, and images with the intent to unlearn and produce student texts of resistance and cultural production. With that in mind I want to support this emerging teaching paradigm with some description and analysis of my own teaching.

MY PEDAGOGY

In the not too distant past, teaching from a critical pedagogical stance simply meant opening students' eyes to the general inequities related to schools. Often, lecture, roundtable dialogue, some group work, and a lot of student complaining that I was too critical or the readings were too difficult became the backbone of most undergraduate and, at times, graduate foundations courses. This description, of course, does not do full justice to the impact I may have had on some students. On a simple level, my students were at least guided to think critically about schools, which, most of them argued, was more than many of their courses in education were giving them.

As I was developing my theoretical skills, this form of teaching became increasingly problematic. First, I was presenting critical theory in education merely from a position of despair. Using the postmodern theoretical framework as a medium to critically respond to school, incessant deconstruction around difference, marginality, and otherness simply had my students' heads ringing. To what end, they argued, is all this analysis? It's my right as a professor and activist to intellectualize, to be a public intellectual, I would inwardly retort! But my students had a good point. Lost in my ongoing teaching and analysis was a unifying of both the modernistic sets of discussions around freedom, equality, and emancipatory hope and the postmodern deconstruction around difference that would render hope even possible. In moving between the dialectic of structural despair and hope, I have needed to find an outlet that would on some theoretical and practical level present the "critical" message as one that is always in flux, and not simply deterministically caught in "catch 22" traps of cultural reproduction. Popular culture has become an outlet in which to work this out both theoretically as well as practically.

Sadly, perhaps, what is missing in Giroux's *Disturbing Pleasures* is an argument for more student narrative about both their own subjugated oppressions and popular culture connections. Before writing exercises "take on" critical popular cultural elements, such as that of Giroux, it seems to me that students first have to come to terms with their own complicitness within the culture they are learning to critique.

As a result of this, I often start class with a personal narrative that places me in a privileged culture. I talk about my particular historical construction as a Jew growing up, as an immigrant in Israel and the United States. I talk about my alienating school experiences, my patriarchal experiences involving parents and schools, and so on. In short, I expose students to the pain I have felt growing up as both a conspirator and victim of the culture I lived in (Kanpol, 1994). Of course, this all relates to the movies I watched on television while growing up, the advertisements I remember, and the music I listened to. Subsequently, using my narrative as a model, I ask students to recover what Welch (1985) calls "dangerous memories," in an effort to come to terms with their historically constructed, oppressed, and privileged past. This necessarily involves them also talking about the movies they watched while growing up, the books they read in school, the Disney movies they enjoyed at the theater, the kind of clothes they wore as students, the music they listened to, and other popular images they come up with.

This exercise, which usually lasts at least one three-hour session, and at times more, is meant to accomplish at least two things. First, as a professor I am situating myself in a vulnerable position. Essentially I am relating to students that I am part of the social problem I am attempting to challenge. I am also historically constructed. This kind of pedagogy begins to break down the patriarchal, authoritative gap between professor and student. Second, this exercise is meant to entice students out of their uncriticality and into a position in which they can begin to feel the historical criticality they can have if they begin to view popular culture as a medium for understanding their personal lives. Despair and hope play hand in hand as students begin to reconstruct their now former social amnesia with "popular" possibilities!

This "popular" pulse is the beginning point at which to understand the critical elements of educational theory that formerly guided my lecture, overhead, discussion, and some group work in previous years. Through narrative and popular culture, the tone has been set by students in an unauthoritative way to explore their own subjectivities and identity constructions. As a teacher, I merely become the guide in exploring popular moments in students' history that would help them unravel the masked "realities" of their past.

What must be clearly emphasized here is that popular culture in my classroom becomes an ongoing medium that I refer to throughout my foundations courses. In some sense, it becomes the defining element to all "critical" theoretical points I make. For instance, I often refer and am critical of the "American Dream" by discussing the affective investments (emotional responses and effects) in the movies *Rocky* or *Forest Gump*. The illusion of social mobility and social class will be discussed as related to *Officer and Gentleman* as well as *Pretty Woman* and *To Sir With Love*. Machismo will be related to the advertisement of the old Marlboro ad as well as connected to violence in the *Rambo* series and *Pulp Fiction*. Sexuality will be publicly, and if need be, personally analyzed and scrutinized through the movies *Working Woman, Basic Instinct, Pretty Woman, Fatal Attraction*, and *Disclosure*. Male dominance and sexism will be connected to old sitcoms such as *All in the Family* (Archie Bunker),

Father Knows Best, and *Happy Days*. Multiple personalities and socially constructed identities will be discussed during the semester and referenced to the movies *Breakfast Club* and *Pump up the Volume*.

As the semester unfolds, these historically ideological constructions will be discussed in conjunction with Disney movies such as *Aladdin, Beauty and the Beast*, and *The Lion King*, as well as racism in movies such as *Good Morning Vietnam* and *Grand Canyon*, among others. In other words, educational history with its social construction (social efficiency, racism, classism, and gender inequities) must be connected to popular culture for history and make even more sense for my students. As a class, students also bring advertisements to describe the various oppressive social structures *still* in operation. We view some of *The Dead Poet's Society* and *Stand and Deliver*, which both support and/or challenge these structures. I have students construct their own film or bring in film clips such as *Romero* depicting social struggle guided by personal faith and social activism. Theoretically, there is a movement between the despair of social inequity within popular culture and the joy of constructing alternative visions.

All the above occurs during class time over such issues as the hidden curriculum and within a broad social analysis using various aspects of postmodernism, feminism, colonialism, postcolonialism, and poststructuralism. I emphatically add that all this is related to the everyday world of teachers, their students, and both their historical makeups. Nothing could better depict this than this past summer, when my in-service teachers connected popular culture, patriarchy, sexism, and a conservative right agenda to the firing of a progressive superintendent of one of Harrisburg's larger school districts. In short, popular culture is a medium that allows students the space to struggle for a more just, caring, and compassionate world. This is the beginning hope and joy that they view popular culture with.

CONCLUSION

I started this chapter by reemphasizing the moribund conditions of teacher education in this country. I claimed that a new and emerging qualitative form of inquiry such as popular culture can be a vehicle used to challenge oppressive hegemonic constructions. As a conclusion, I extend this argument on a more theoretical level.

For too long now critical educationalists have mired themselves in a nihilistic criticism of educational institutions. The "postmodern" bandwagon has been jumped on in such ways as to lose sight of the modern narratives of justice, freedom, and hope for an enlightenment ideal. Although I have made this argument before in various ways (Kanpol, in press), I emphasize here that the left's gloom and doom or as I have previously called it, "cynicism and despair," must be juxtaposed to move dialectically with what I have also called "joy and hope." This is precisely where I believe Giroux's view of the public intellectual can help us. It is important to note here that popular culture from a deconstructionist (postmodern) position can only be viewed from a cynical and despairing perspective as it relates to social structural doom if it is not connected to the affective investments that arouse intellectual and practical possibility out of this doom.

On a deeper level, this is what Giroux offers his readers. This is what I try to "get at" in my foundation's classes. This is not an argument for becoming the teacher technician who simply turns on the television or radio switch to view popular culture. In a very sophisticated way, Giroux, invests in the *affective investments* of his readers so as to raise their consciousness to the doom and gloom of the present hegemonic social structural conditions. What Giroux succeeds in doing on an even deeper level is to create the joy and hope for both my socially committed students as well as those who have not been "awakened" by a critical calling, that would render being a transformative intellectual *more* feasible, that would open avenues to student voices *more* probable, and that would insert politics into pedagogy even *more* understandable. Simply, Giroux skillfully moves between the critical cynic and hopeful artist in connecting the best of postmodern's deconstruction with the best of modernism's quest for a more unified vision of enlightenment ideals. *This* is how my students view Giroux's work. This is one of the theoretical structures I attempt to also teach out of, and this is a part of the paradigmatic shift that teaching for a new paradigm in teacher education presupposes. Simply put, this paradigm shift also presupposes that students will become consumers of culture, criticalists who in their consumption will intellectualize over the possibilities to create alternative visions.

Perhaps I have not done justice to the power of Giroux's text. I say this because as all criticalists know, a text should *not* be represented for the mere words embedded between the front and back covers. On that simple level, Giroux has deconstructed well the harmful effects that popular culture has in the everyday world. To reiterate, Giroux goes right to the heart of the "affect" as he allows students to deconstruct their own internal investments into the popular, with an eye to challenging students to take in the popular as a theoretical terrain for an emancipatory struggle. In my mind, that connected with the narrative forms and the continual investment of popular culture as a text and teaching tool has the potential to emerge as an alternate teaching paradigm[1] we can learn and grow from, one that undermines the dominant and oppressive teaching paradigm that teacher education has historically constructed for us.

CLASSROOM ACTIVITIES

1. Listen to portions of talk radio such as Rush Limbaugh. Discuss his politics, vision, and agenda for America. Do the same with the people who call in. Connect them to "popular culture."
2. As a homework activity, watch a movie or sitcom. Discuss the race, class, and gender issues emanating as the politics of this aspect of popular culture.
3. A class activity, take the role of the qualitative researcher and use this research methodology to view, take notes on, and interact with what you perceive the culture to be at your university.
4. Watch snippets of Disney animated films. Have each group analyze a portion of the film in light of "popular culture."

QUESTIONS FOR DISCUSSION

1. What role did popular culture play in your past?
   a. How did popular culture "mobilize" your sentiments?
2. How have you been implicated in the dominant popular culture both theoretically and practically? Cite examples.
3. What role will your curriculum have (if any) if it is connected to popular culture?
4. Discuss the differences between conservative and liberal talk shows? Compare this with the movies Talk Radio and Good Morning Vietnam.

---

[1]By this I mean that popular culture does not simply have to remain in social foundations courses. It can also be incorporated into other foundation's courses such as learning theory courses, teaching strategy courses, and other areas that connect teaching to the everyday world of students.

REFERENCES

Britzman, D. (1991). *Practice makes practice*. Albany: State University of New York Press.

Fine, M. (1988). Sexuality, schooling, and adolescent females: The missing discourse of desire. *Harvard Educational Review, 58*, 29-53.

Giroux, H. (1988). *Teachers as intellectuals*. Westport, CT: Bergin & Garvey.

Giroux, H. (1994). *Disturbing pleasures: Learning popular culture*. New York: Routledge.

Giroux, H. (1995a). Talk radio, public intellectuals and right wing pedagogy. *The Cultural Studies Times, 1*, 3, Fall.

Giroux, H. (1995b). Animating youth: The disneyfication of children's culture. *Socialist Review, 24*(3), 23-55.

Grossberg, L. (1992). *We gotta get out of this place*. New York: Routledge.

hooks, b. (1994). *Teaching to transgress: Education as the practice of freedom*. New York: Routledge.

Kanpol, B. (1994). *Critical pedagogy: An introduction*. Westport, CT: Bergin & Garvey.

Kanpol, B. (in press). *Teachers talking back and breaking bread*. Cresskill, NJ: Hampton Press.

Kincheloe, J. (1993). *Toward a critical politics of teacher thinking: Mapping the postmodern*. Westport, CT: Bergin & Garvey.

Kozol, J. (1991). *Savage inequalities*. New York: Crown.

Kuhn, T. (1970). *The structure of scientific revolutions*. Urbana: University of Illinois Press.

Noddings, N. (1992). *The challenge to care in schools: An alternative approach to education*. New York: Teachers College Press.

McLaren, P. (1994). *Life in schools*. New York: Longman.

Weiner, L. (1993). *Preparing teachers for urban schools: Lessons from 30 years of school reform*. New York: Teacher's College Press.

Welch, S. (1985). *Communities of resistance and solidarity: A feminist theology of creation*. New York: Orbis Books.

Yeo, F. (1996). *Classrooms of the inner city: Urban education, teacher education, search for new connections*. New York: Garland Press.

9

Outcome-Based Education and Democratic Commitment: Hopes and Possibilities

A Poem From A Preservice Student
on the State of Teacher Education

The Messengers

There'll be food on the table tonight
for the henchmen and his crew
they've sifted through the many
to finally arrive at the few.
The bulk of the resistance,
though locked away in our minds,
left a trail of destruction
evidence for ignorance to find.
They seized us in a procession
a carpe diem battle cry,
critical unity for the masses
yet in a single irony did we die.
Beaten and naked they did drag us
through the market place of repent,
a feeble form of market oppression
seeking conformity and consent.
But years of witnessing to the deaf

had muted our voices into silence
where none of their martyred atrocities
could ever vocalize our compliance.
And though bloodied were our bodies,
our hearts and souls sustained,
persistent warriors against the dogma
carried by the church's socially insane.
And the dark gallows they did tremble
as they stole our breaths away,
lifting the weights upon our shoulders
in an effort to mold them in their way.
But our messages could not be altered
or destroyed they eventually did find,
for our messages are locked away safely
in the expanses of our minds,
taken with us into the mystic,
above the wonder, across the divide,
forever linked into obscurity,
forever lost to the other side.

This poem from a former undergraduate student of mine depicts how he feels as the deskilled in-service teacher. However readers interpret the poem, one sure bet is that there is despair being sent out as a messenger and having been deskilled. The hopeful sign, of course, is that students like the one who wrote this poem (anonymous) will act as cultural workers to instill hope into a system that has historically been stigmatized by social efficiency.

Clearly, I have also depicted the field of teacher education to be problematic. An earlier chapter by Fred Yeo indicated, perhaps like some of the poem's messages, that teacher education in general does not prepare its clientele for the multiple realities of daily teaching, especially in urban schools. The previous chapter argued for teacher education to be more progressive in its thinking by helping form teachers into public intellectuals who are committed to a democratic citizenry. Clearly, popular culture is not the only terrain that teacher education and teachers in general must struggle with for a "critical" politics to rear its head.

For too long now, it seems to me, reform in the education field has exacerbated a one-sided, power-based capitalistic enterprise (Apple, 1988; Shapiro, 1985). Coupled with this dominating and at times oppressive ideology, schools have been subject to rigid structures of teacher and student accountability and behavioristic learning outcomes. As has been argued time and again in this book, social efficiency has been the dominating paradigm in which hegemonically constructed values articulated through the hidden curriculum (Anyon, 1980; Fine, 1991; Kanpol, 1992; McLaren, 1994; Weiler, 1988; Willis, 1977) have portrayed the typical critical theory dilemma of "reproductive theory." That is, on the one hand, there is a tendency in schools for teachers and/or students to culturally resist oppressive structures of race, class, gender, and other institutional dominant forms. Yet, on the other hand, these acts of resistance have often led to an accommodation to these same oppressive social structures, such as Willis's (1977) study on the "Lads," among others. Seemingly caught in a "Catch 22" syndrome, some critical theorists in education have turned to the postmodern (otherwise also termed poststructural) literature as a theoretical referent to challenge the social realities that critical theory in education has uncovered and problematized within its theories about school social structures.

     This is not the place to explicate on a totality of postmodern theories. In education, theorists such as Giroux (1992, 1993), Shapiro (1989), Burbules and Rice (1991), Lather (1991), Kincheloe and Steinberg (1993), Kanpol and McLaren (1995), Peters (1995), and a growing host of others have portrayed the problematic of "difference" in a multiethnic society. Multiculturalists, as discussed in an earlier chapter, would also agree with these theorists (Grant & Sachs, 1995; Nieto, 1992, among many others). To reiterate one basic argument of this book; these theorists' basic premise is that school clientele (teachers and students) can no longer rely on singular truth or one reality for knowledge. That would be too *socially efficient* of a mindset. Texts, they argue, have multiple interpretations, especially given the specific context of the reader. Difference is problematized to include multiple subjectivities, identities, and realities. Taking issue with this literature as it relates to educational reform can be an arduous task. For, how does one even write "postmodern" policy, if it can only be perceived on a multirealitied level? Or, how can one write an outcome (as in the *Outcome-Based Education* [OBE] reform) in postmodern terms, knowing that, at best, a singular outcome can only be interpreted in postmodern multiple senses?

     With this in mind, it was interesting to read Capper and Jamison's (1993) recent article in *Educational Policy.* Their thesis was that OBE merely reproduces the dominant power structures, particularly if OBE is viewed through a structural-functional paradigm. Their final contention, however, is hopeful. If OBE could be viewed through the lens of alternative epistemological perspectives, such as critical theory or postmodernism, there may be a chance that emancipatory structures can exist as a part of reform policies. My main task in this chapter then is to build on this provocative assumption by hypothesizing what postmodern theorizing would look like as policy, knowing well that even this attempt is contradictory to the postmodern condition (Lyotard, 1984). To do this, however, is also an attempt to gear postmodernists along with other criticalists in education to a committed, visionary and concrete reality, a grounded form of democratic hope within difference. I first theorize about this possibility. Second, I outline what these principles might look like. I then translate this into practical teacher possibilities through OBE examples. In conclusion, I discuss what this may mean for teacher education departments in general.

CRITICAL THEORY AND POSTMODERNISM

Educational critical theorists concerned with democratic hopes and possibilities have often fallen into theorizing about social despair and hopelessness. Even though resistance theorists have portrayed culturally productive hope, the inevitable social and cultural reproductive trap has been typically couched within capitalistic structures. For example let's revisit Willis's (1977) study. The Lads' celebration of defying school institutional logic succumbed them to replicate manual labor and patriarchal relations, and further their subordinate social positions. Anyon's (1980) study, despite possibilities of resistance, merely subordinated students to tracked social class divisions. McLaren's (1994) illuminating teaching experiences admittedly pushed him to reconsider how he merely reinforced dominant and oppressive ideological values, despite his liberal teaching style. Fine's (1991) study depicted how female voices are muted. Weiler's (1988) study shows how female teachers' voices in schools struggle to find room for expression. Britzman's (1991) study shows us how difficult it is for student teachers to find their resistant voice, and Kanpol's (1992) studies depicted only fleeting moments of emancipatory hope and possibility.

In these cases (and there are many more), Marxist and Neo-Marxist theories of production predominate. In an economically differentiated economy, there is a clear division of labor. Schools divide their clientele into social slots, with minimal hopes of social transformation. Comprehensive studies such as Oakes's (1985) work on tracking and Kozol's (1991) recent work on social inequity provide deep and explicit evidence that the institution of school is far from a democratic hubris, despite some critical theorists' attempts to challenge this notion.

This literature has been attacked for its lack of emancipatory possibilities. Postmodernists in education, in particular, have been involved in theorizing about difference, identity, and subjectivity. Assuming the mantle of postmodern theorizing, many critical theorists have begun to deconstruct difference on multiple levels. For instance, Giroux (1992) has brilliantly combined feminist, postmodern, and modern literature and literature of and about minority writers into a comprehensive argument for schools to create "borders" of understanding. Giroux's argument is that there can be no one totalizing theory for schools, given the different and floating identity that individuals own. Yet, there can be, he argues, unities of border understandings that may challenge oppressive institutional structures that lead to student-centered "critical" learning. This, Giroux argues, may lead to furthering the critical democratic left agenda. Postmodern feminists (Ellsworth, 1989; Gordon, 1995; Lather, 1989, 1991) have argued that difference is so multiple that there cannot be one owner of truth. Thus, each individual's identity has its own truths and moments of emancipation from oppression, subordination, and domination. Kincheloe and Steinberg (1993) have argued that teacher education departments must reach beyond traditional ways of thinking about cognitive structures. They argue for "postformal" thinking, a "critical constructivism," the capacity not merely to think in the Bloomian six-step linear cognitive sense, but to apply this knowledge to both understand and challenge social structures within new ways of knowing.

Multiculturalists in and out of education have also typically fallen into "reproductive" traps, at once depicting the inequity of the educational system, but concurrently lacking any comprehensive theory, practice, and policy to provide democratic support to challenge older, oppressive, and subordinative structures (Pierce, 1995). Although this is not the place to divulge all theories of multiculturalism (all of which possess borders of either conservative, liberal, or radical forms), as indicated in Chapter 4, what is clear is that schools are typically held accountable to some form of multicultural difference, even if difference obfuscates the division of cultures into race, class, and gender disparities.

I have argued elsewhere (Kanpol, 1992, 1994) that if educators in and out of public schools are to gain emancipatory and/or critical ground, theory, practice, and policy must be interrelated into a comprehensive framework. Sometimes caught myself within postmodern theorizing, I have previously called for a "democratic imaginary" to guide what it might look like for "difference" to similarly challenge oppressive social forms. In my earlier works I have struggled and only minimally succeeded to frame this notion into a comprehensive package; rightly so, according to critical theorists and postmodern writers. For who can determine all norms and values in the context of any educational framework? Like Giroux (1992), I have argued for unity across difference. That is, as a postmodern challenge to educational policymakers, I find it intriguing to attempt to formulate what policy would look like within an emancipatory framework. A step forward in this direction has been my reading of much of the liberation theologists outside of education. For instance, West (1993) argues that prophetic thought is different from traditional academic discourse. Fighting injustice, for example, must be connected to doing the right thing by returning to one's faith for guidance in action. Of course, this idea would be intolerable to mention as an outcome in any policy statement. The question then becomes: To whose faith does one return to undo social ills?

This dilemma poses major problems for policymakers. OBE has been hit severely by the far right (religious and non-religious) for its supposed vague outcomes regarding "appreciating and understanding others," "tolerance of differences," and "respect for diversity" (McQuaide & Pliska, 1993). The far left have criticized policymakers for providing a pseudo-liberal document that merely covers up who controls constructing outcomes and not really dealing with social inequity (Capper & Jamison, 1993). Lacking in the document, it seems to me, is that the issue of democracy is lost within a sea of objectives, behavioristically defined, sequentially substantiated, and with little room to explore alternative meanings. Capper and Jamison forcefully argue that the interest of OBE is not to transform but to merely stabilize, to cover up the really oppressive inequalities of school in the guise that "all" students can succeed. In this catch-all statement, it would be fair to argue that not all students could succeed to be Michael Jordon or Albert Einstein. That some students can succeed on different levels is a possibility. Capper and Jamison's (1993) point is well taken: "Thus, even though OBE claims to embrace all students, the principles and practices of OBE may exclude students with disabilities, especially students with cognitive disabilities" (p. 439).

We have come to a point, then, that what defines success becomes a major issue. Additionally, what normative framework that is democratic and inclusive of difference and that could also be workable amidst epistemological uncertainties becomes my guide to be able to theoretically and practically account for educational reform. In the following section I expand this argument on two levels. I outline what a critical, postmodern teaching or learning process might look like epistemologically. I then translate this process into what I perceive educational outcomes to be, using as my base some of OBE's tenets.

THE LEARNING PROCESS "CRITICALLY" AND "POSTMODERN" DEFINED

It is worth repeating that simply entering a learning principle seems contradictory in the face of postmodern theorizing. At best, one can take these guiding principles within a broad critical framework and attempt to formulate an educational agenda that has democratic imperatives as its core.

Stainback and Stainback (1992), as outlined by Capper and Jamison (1993), presented behavioristic/reductionistic as opposed to holistic/constructivist teaching and learning principles and processes. Critical theorists would argue that although constructing a holistic learning experience is good in and of itself, it does not commit to the democratic imaginary I outlined earlier or even to John Dewey's social democratic imaginary outlined many years ago. Thus, this progressive, liberal formulation (holistic learning process) does not enter into the critical sphere to alter the behavioral model of learning that schools have been hegemonized into. In the following I add to the 12 principles of a constructivist learning paradigm, knowing that an emancipatory learning process includes constructivist learning processes but lacks critical and postmodern outlets.

Principles of the Holistic Constructivist Teaching and Learning Process Versus Principles of a Critical Democratic Teaching and Learning Process

1. The whole of the learned experience is greater than the sum of its parts.
   versus
1. The whole learned experience is divided by parts reflected on as a part of different student social experiences.
2. The interaction of the learned experience transforms both the individual's spiral (whole) and the single experience (part).
   versus
2. The interaction of the learned experience transforms individuals's spiral and single experience as related to similar and different social experiences (whole and part).
3. The learner's spiral of knowledge is self-regulating and self-preserving.
   versus
3. The learner's spiral of knowledge self-regulates and self-preserves as it directly relates to personal experiences and the learning process.

4. All people are learners actively searching for and constructing new meanings.

versus

4. All learners search for and conduct personal meanings and experiences as related to institutional and social structures that connect them to race, class, and gender.

5. The best predictor of how someone will learn is what he or she already knows.

versus

5. Learning prediction is never complete, as experience and knowledge is ongoing, changing, and in flux.

6. The development of accurate forms follows the emergence of function and meaning.

versus

6. Accurate forms are the function of ongoing meaning making by the student and teacher in an dialectical process of inquiry that is nonthreatening and nonauthoritarian.

7. Learning often proceeds from whole to part to whole.

versus

7. Learning is defined by its incomplete nature as whole as experience is always meaning negotiated.

8. Errors are critical to learning.

versus

8. Errors relate both to learning and the socialization process of values such as competition, success, and teamwork.

9. Learners learn best from experiences in which they are passionately involved.

versus

9. Learners learn best from dispositional interests mixed with normative judgment, democratically negotiated between higher school authorities, teachers, parent groups, and student representatives.

10. Learners learn best from people they trust.

versus

10. Learners learn best when trust is a function of identity understanding and negotiation.

11. Experiences connected to the learner's present knowledge and interest are learned best.

versus

11. Experiences connected to the learners present knowledge about social conditions as related to race, class, gender, age, and so on prompt the learning interest level to rise.

12. Integrity is a primary characteristic of the human (learner's) mind.

versus

12. Integrity as a learner's mind condition is connected in and out of the schools, is experience based, identity driven, and different for every student.

OBE AND POSTMODERN POSSIBILITIES

No doubt, the debate surrounding OBE and its value-sidedness or seeming neutrality is another way of visualizing the competing knowledge-believing and -constructing constituencies made up in American society. Despite the fact that part of the original goal no. 6—"attitudes and behavior" was eliminated from the official document, any fair-minded teacher, professor in education, or school official will admit that attitudes and behavior are what schools really invest in. We have learned through the literature on the "hidden curriculum" that this is precisely the case. I have often argued to my educational foundations students that, in large part, most of our "social" teaching is filtered through the hidden curriculum. To deny that attitudes and behaviors should be taught in schools is to obfuscate the school's function to filter values into the curriculum. This is what made Dewey's argument of continuity between school and society and the child and curriculum so compelling. There is and always must be a connection if experience is to be understood. Without this understanding, education and democracy could not be embraced for Dewey. Schools as terrains of social struggle and meaning making will also explicitly be a part of teacher and administrative struggle of difference, catering around these issues of values and experiences.

Capper and Jamison (1993) are correct with their claim that OBE outcomes can never embrace all students. They see through OBE's contradictions (OBE purports to remove time barriers, yet curriculum objectives are set for specific grade levels). Lacking within Capper and Jamison's argument, however, is the role that postmodern theorizing can play in the everyday life world of the classroom. Although this is not the time nor the place to make practical all school activities, there is room for some discussion on how the principles of critical democratic teaching and learning processes outlined earlier may be played out in a school and understood by teachers through OBE.

EPISTEMOLOGY AND THE PRACTICAL

In general, the 12 democratic principles relate in some ways to Dewey's notions of experience. Dewey's pragmatism in the classroom setting allows curriculum to be flexible, student centered, and contextually bound. Importantly for Dewey, the school is a form of public sphere. Thus, learning experiences as I have outlined earlier, should be related dialectically to structural configurations such as race, class, and gender. Meaning for postmodernists and Dewey is always negotiated as a form of on-going and ever-changing dialectics. For instance, school and student, experience and reflection, experience and learning, experience and meaning, interest and experience, identity and experience, and race, class, gender, and experience are all integrally related in fluid constructions of student general experiences and meaning making. For Dewey, this was integrally related to education and democracy.

Critical to a democratic platform is an epistemology that takes seriously the issue of human agency in the meaning-making process. The principles outlined earlier call for student free-thinking in light of experience, as connected to the social world. Thus, democracy can only be defined by a teacher-learner dialectic around the issues of experience and personal and social identity—a reflection on what Mead (1934) would call the self and generalized other (internalized norms).

Democracy, then, involves students deconstructing personal and public experiences that also relate to oppression, alienation, and subordination. Democratic teaching prompts a raising of student interest and consciousness levels of experience as connected to various forms of public life. Additionally, democratic teaching negotiates authority as an ongoing dialectic—teacher and students as co-authors of knowledge, co-authorities of narrative and experience in negotiation and confrontation with the curriculum, be it the social sciences, humanities, or the sciences. Democratic participation in the curriculum necessarily means an understanding of the curriculum as it directly relates to the personal and the public. In addition, how the personal and the public are understood on multiple levels is vital. That is, how the personal and public are connected to institutions of wealth, poverty, racism, and gender must be understood both experientially and theoretically for the teaching-learning process to be democratic.

As a part of this epistemology of democracy, schools must embrace its tenets at all times and in all forms to ensure student and teacher full participation. Furthermore, a democratic epistemology, is not innocent or devoid of values. Unlike the "holistic" epistemological experience, which is basically noncommittal politically, an innocent bystander of experience, a liberal ideal that simply challenges behaviorism's reductionistic teacher-learning process, the democratic teaching/learning process is value laden, subjectively driven, politically loaded, and normatively based. Put differently, democracy requires the utmost commitment from teachers and students to undo social ills, create new and vital borders of meanings, open spaces for alternative interpretations, and leave room for justice and human dignity. In a democratic epistemology there cannot be any form of indifference to experience and reflection. Tied to ongoing negotiation, experience and reflection must begin to signify connections to race, class, and gender, as connected to history, literature, geography, popular culture forms, and so on.

Moreover, this democratic vision becomes for teachers and students lived experiences, a way of living, or, even, commonsensical daily experiences. Like the behavioristic model or other forms of technocratic rationality, rather than conform to a stultified vision of teaching and learning as commonsensical and hegemonic, a democratic platform attempts to reverse the former stagnant trend by first understanding its ramifications and then transforming that model to be commonsensical. Democracy becomes the ideal or the imaginary. Behaviorism is nullified. Furthermore, holistic experience is made *more meaningful* in light of democratic hopes and possibilities.

OUTCOME-BASED EDUCATION AND DEMOCRATIC POSSIBILITIES

One could review all 53 outcomes, deconstruct them for democratic possibilities, and be done with it. This is not, however, my intent. Some education professors have approached me with the question: "Isn't outcomes-based education critical theory?" My response has always been with much caution. Although not wanting to offend colleagues, I have commented simply: "It depends on how any single teacher approaches any single outcome." I argue that outcomes-based education can be critical depending on the political position of the teacher(s) adopting its program. Democratic possibilities and outcomes-based education then, for me, has democratic hopes in two ways: (a) the public debate and their particular controversies, and (b) particular outcomes. I next give one example of both to amplify the democratic epistemological points I made earlier.

The biggest public controversy over OBE came when a values component—Outcome No. 6—said that "Appreciating and Understanding Others" was viewed as "teaching values." Under Outcome No. 6 it was explicated that "all students explore and articulate the similarities and differences among various cultures and the history and contributions of diverse cultural groups, including groups to which they belong."

This value component was challenged by various constituencies, claiming that appreciating and understanding others would promote a value system different from the students' own. Interestingly, the argument is a seemingly democratic one. That is, all constituencies have a right to argue their political position. More fundamentally, however, the political argument over values from the more fundamental right and left obfuscates the deeper democratic issues having to do with the issues of race, class and gender disparities, inner-city inequities, and the general condition of declining public education possibilities for many minority youth (Kozol, 1991) and youth apathy (Gaines, 1992). Rather than argue over issues of common democratic hopes and dreams, and the schools' ability to challenge the causes of social ills and inequities, the values debate, although holding some democratic merit, was politically charged with value one-sidedness, instead of value inclusiveness. Again, the democratic hope lies within the debate and differences of values that are exuded. What is to be done with these differences, however, becomes the basis for democratic possibility.

Despite the debate and different value constituencies, ultimately, democratic hopes particularly lie within the four walls of the classroom with the teacher. What the teacher does with particular outcomes will reflect on his or her epistemological framework (Kanpol, 1994). Take for instance a born-again Christian teacher's philosophy (a student in one of my graduate foundation's classes) and one general outcome I deconstruct. This teacher, who is head of his school's science department, commented:

> I wanted a career that would serve God, so I could be an example to others. While I can never preach my faith to kids, I can encourage them to identify common values, identify their own voices, to communicate with differences. Many students respond well to this caring attitude. I urge students to question the foundations of their beliefs.

This caring philosophy is carried across to curricular issues as well:

> As we contemplate a new curriculum for our lowest academic level of science (homogenous tracked students) I see signs of a staff weary

of the struggle of dealing with disinterested students. Apathy among the students comes not from a boring text. It stems from recognizing a staff member who shows little interest in making a curriculum that involves the life of the students. These students need pragmatic experiences that allow them to see the importance of science education in their lives. This type of curriculum does not come from a textbook. It stems from recognizing a staff member who identifies with student needs and adjusts daily activities to those needs. I argue for a course that will involve student choices in science: a course that will attract students of varying academic abilities and gender. Such a course must involve student projects, internships, and other pragmatic views of science to ensure a phenomonological and critical relationship between the student and the curriculum.

Clearly, this teacher teaches from a phenomonological viewpoint—understanding student voices and histories from students' perspective. This viewpoint makes the holistic epistemology more feasible. For this teacher, science is not necessarily behavioristic because it includes the experiences of the whole child. From a more critical tradition or, as I have termed it, a critical teaching, democratic learning process, this teacher is committed for "females to become chemistry teachers in a male-dominated profession," to "connect experiences in a non-authoritarian way while still claiming to be an authority, "to care and share with students so as to understand their experiences in light of their world." Clearly, despite any internal faith agreements or disagreements, this teacher (from his viewpoint as a cultural worker for God) is working to undermine dominant values of authoritarianism, a stagnant, standardized curriculum and gender bias, and so on. Within his phenomenology and holistic experiences, he has personally taken on semblances of a critical democratic teaching-learning platform.

As a committed educator seeking justice and the end to forms of oppression, I am interested in how teachers (such as the ones above) struggle to participate within a universal sensibility to achieve results that a democratic educational platform could engulf. Within the democratic principles outlined earlier, I refer in particular to OBE's democratic possibilities. What I have established (and of no surprise here) is that it is the individual teacher who has the control and power to initiate democratic reform through particular subjective readings of outcomes. Critically important about this educational reform is that it allows teachers both the personal autonomy and time to accomplish a particular outcome. So, although *formal* Outcome No. 9 under *citizenship* requires that "all students understand the history and nature of prejudice and relate their knowledge to current issues facing communities, the United States and other nations," the path is open for teachers to experiment with democratic forms of education, under the rubric of democratic principles I previously outlined earlier.

Additionally, although the struggle still exists over Outcome No. 6 and its moral fabric, "to appreciate and understand others," the struggle is over one democratic possibility—hopes and dreams, or real people's experiences. Of course one could argue that various constituencies like the far religious right or liberal left schools have their own agenda. Nothing could be truer. More importantly, however, is to view this struggle as one for curricular space; a common struggle over faith concerns, beliefs, and attitudes; and a search for values that would make the social world a qualitatively better place. OBE becomes the terrain in which democracy can unfold and in which the postmodern multiple real-life experiences take shape and form in light of a common democratic school agenda.

Unlike many critical theorists who will *only* deconstruct pitfalls of OBE, I take the stand that there are democratic possibilities, particularly if teachers are ready to take an epistemological democratic teaching-learning process stance in their subject matter—a position that challenges forms of oppression, alienation and subordination.

CONCLUSIONS: WHAT HAS THIS TO DO WITH TEACHER EDUCATION?

I have described earlier in this book and elsewhere (Kanpol, 1994) how my personal teaching experiences in public schools, my teaching certification program, and the state's official curriculum regulations and guidelines *never* coincided, but seemed to contradict on another. As a beginning teacher, this confused me greatly. Although there has been literature on this issue, and particularly about the travails of first-year teachers, it seems to me that if teacher education departments do not combine higher level theory and practice, much of the same kind of technocratic, unknowing, and naive teacher will be reproduced.

Often a haven for producing the "practical" teacher, the teacher equipped with a discipline plan, a lesson plan with a sea of objectives, and so on teacher education departments, by their very "practical" mindset, have been de-intellectualized. They do not produce the public intellectual Giroux and others are advocating. The argument to theorize more in teacher education is not new. However, I want to take the view that theorizing should take on a particular stand.

Teacher education departments must now intellectualize over how theory and practice can be combined between high schools and universities. That is, to claim a holistic philosophy or, even further, a democratic philosophy in preparing students, strident efforts must be made to democratize teacher education departments. This means intense dialogue over competing views on what counts as knowledge, experience, and identity.

Although views may (and will) differ, the effort must be made to create borders of understanding that include some of the democratic principles mentioned earlier. Clearly, teacher education departments can set the tone for students to emulate in public schools, if they hold true to a democratic, rather than an autocratic and purely technocratic, platform. The gap between theorizing and practice is not necessarily built on how to practicalize Madeline Hunter, Skinner, Piaget, or Bloom. Rather, gaps between theory and practice can be built around democratic principles. Closing the gap is dependent on a teacher education department's ability to create its own strategic democratic outcome-based education. Closing the gap between schools and teacher education department's emulation of similar outcome-based objectives may lead to further investigation on how outcomes, once defined, can be both practical and concurrently theoretically loaded within a democratic vision. Of course, this means honest and open dialogue, and less bureaucracy in department meetings, serious commitment to teacher education departments as sites of social and cultural transformation, and a compelling vision for preservice teachers based on democratic principles, hopes, and dreams.

It seems to me that only when teacher education departments combine with schools to dialogue over outcome-based education can a democratic vision even be visualized. Before this can occur, the gap between the practical nature of schools and the technocratic nature of teacher education departments must be openly scrutinized for its pitfalls. I first argue for teacher education departments to create outcomes that would challenge existing technocratic and oppressive race, class, and gender disparities. I then call for outcomes to be scrutinized for their democratic intent. How they play within the practical walls of foundations and strategies classes must be connected for the theoretical policy to be made more pragmatic. It seems feasible to have superintendents, principals, teachers, and other school personnel join in the discussion with teacher education professors.

Clearly, democracy must be made both an explicit outcome and be incorporated into the formal and "hidden" curriculum if we are to make headway to deal with the undoing of the "savage inequalities" Kozol (1991) writes about. As institutions of change, schools in general and districts in particular have the opportunity through outcome-based education to make a "social" impact. This impact, however, can only be made feasible if borders of understanding, a commitment to democracy, and a challenge to older epistemological frameworks be both challenged and transformed.

CLASSROOM ACTIVITIES

1. In groups, research older school reforms (no-matter how far back they go) and discuss their ramifications for schools. Connect these reforms to both social efficiency and critical pedagogy.
2. In groups, outline what you believe to be the necessary educational reform items needed for a critical citizenry.
3. In group subject areas, construct an outline of a curriculum inclusive of these reforms.
4. Outline for a principal a reform package that justifies democracy (concentrate on your subject area).

QUESTIONS FOR DISCUSSION

1. What does reform mean to you?
2. What did reform look like when you were in high school?
3. What blockades and hopes exist for a democratic reform proposal?
4. What arguments can you give to future teachers (particularly conservatives) on reform of the sort mentioned in this chapter?

REFERENCES

Anyon, J. (1980). Social class and the hidden curriculum of work. *Journal of Education, 162*, 66-92.

Apple, M. (1988). *Teachers and texts*. New York: Routledge & Kegan Paul.

Britzman, D. (1991). *Practice makes practice: A critical study of learning to teach*. Albany: State University of New York Press.

Burbules, N., & Rice, S. (1991). Dialogue across differences: Continuing the conversation. *Harvard Educational Review, 61*(4), 393-416.

Capper, C., & Jamison, M. (1993). Outcomes based education reexamined: From structural functionalism to post structuralism. *Educational Policy, 7*(4), 427-446.

Ellsworth, E. (1989). Why doesn't this feel empowering? Working through the myths of critical pedagogy. *Harvard Educational Review, 59*(3), 29-53.

Fine, M. (1991). *Framing dropouts: Notes on the politics of an urban public high school*. Albany: State University of New York Press.

Gaines, D. (1992). *Teenage wasteland*. New York: HarperCollins .

Giroux, H. (1992). *Border crossings*. New York: Routledge.

Giroux, H. (1993). *Living dangerously*. New York: Peter Lang.

Gordon, B. (1995). Fringe dwellers: African American women in the postmodern. In B. Kanpol & P. McLaren (Eds.), *Critical multiculturalism: Uncommon choices in a common struggle difference* (pp. 59-88). Westport, CT: Bergin & Garvey.

Grant, C., & Sachs, J. (1995). Multicultural education and postmodernism. In B. Kanpol & P. McLaren (Eds.), *Critical multiculturalism: Uncommon choices in a common struggle difference* (pp. 89-106). Westport, CT: Bergin & Garvey.

Kanpol, B. (1992). *Towards a theory and practice of teacher cultural politics*. Norwood, NJ: Ablex.

Kanpol, B. (1994). *Critical pedagogy: An introduction*. Westport, CT: Bergin & Garvey.

Kanpol, B., & McLaren, P. (Eds.). (1995). *Critical multiculturalism: Uncommon voices in a common struggle*. Westport, CT: Bergin & Garvey.

Kincheloe, J., & Steinberg, S. (1993). A tentative description of post-formal thinking: The critical confrontation with cognitive theory. *Harvard Educational Review, 63*(3), 296-320.

Kozol, J. (1991). *Savage inequalities*. New York: Crown Publishers.

Lather, P. (1989). Postmodernism and the politics of enlightenment. *Educational Foundations, 3*, 7-28.

Lather, P. (1991). *Getting smart*. New York: Routledge.

Lyotard, J. (1984). *The postmodern condition: A report on knowledge*. Minneapolis: University of Minnesota Press.

McLaren, P. (1994). *Life in schools*. New York: Longman.

McQuaide, J., & Pliska, A.M. (1993). The challenge to Pennsylvania's education reform. *Educational Leadership, 51*(4), 16-18.

Mead, H. (1934). *Mind, self and society*. Chicago: The University of Chicago Press.

Nieto, S. (1992). *Affirming diversity*. New York: Longman.

Oakes, J. (1985). *Keeping track: How schools structure inequality*. New Haven, CT: Yale University Press.

Peters, M. (Ed.). (1995). *Lyotard and education*. Westport, CT: Bergin & Garvey.

Pierce, B. (1995). Maria's story. In B. Kanpol & P. McLaren (Eds.), *Critical multiculturalism: Uncommon choices in a common struggle difference* (pp. 165-176). Westport, CT: Bergin & Garvey.

Shapiro, S. (1989). Towards a language of educational politics: The struggle for a critical public discourse of education. *Educational Foundations, 3*(3), 79-100.

Shapiro, S. (1985). Capitalism at risk: The political economy of the educational reports of 1983. *Educational Theory, 35*(1), 57-72.

Stainback, W., & Stainback, S. (1992). *Controversial issues confronting special education: Divergent perspectives*. Boston: Allyn and Bacon.

Weiler, K. (1988). *Women teaching for change*. South Hadley, MA: Bergin & Garvey.

West, C. (1993). *Prophetic thought in postmodern times*. Monroe, ME: Common Courage Press.

Willis, P. (1977). *Learning to labor*. Lexington: D.C. Heath.

10

CRITICAL PEDAGOGY AND LIBERATION THEOLOGY IMAGES: BORDERS FOR A TRANSFORMATIVE AGENDA

Praxis is a specific kind of obedience that organizes itself around a social theory of reality in order to implement in the society the freedom, inherent in faith. If faith is the belief in God created all for freedom, then praxis is the social theory used to analyze what must be done for the historical realization of freedom. To sing about freedom and to pray for its coming is not enough. Freedom must be actualized in history by oppressed peoples who accept the intellectual challenge to analyze the world for the purpose of changing it. (Cone, 1986)

The previous chapters have hopefully "whet the appetite" of would-be critical pedagogists. Vital to this critical tradition is to take Cone's words quoted above with the utmost seriousness. Freedom is, in part, the ability to act out of oppression. This particular section in the book on critical pedagogy has indicated, as an *emerging trend,* that this freedom can be viewed spiritually. Perhaps this is a reason why analyzing one's personal narrative is so important. It lends an insight into one's identity and various contradictions and critical junctures. For example, what it means to be a Jew or Christian or any other religion can and does vary, most likely on one's social position. As a concluding chapter, this one level of theology is touched on, particularly as a way to depart from what I term traditional critical pedagogy.

In my mind, the time has come for the educational left, particularly those involved with the critical pedagogy movement, to come to terms with the profound theological possibilities and implications of its work. With the advent of Kozol's (1991) devastating description and critique of inner-city schools in the United States, critical pedagogists in the educational arena have offered much deconstructive analysis of structural school issues around race, class, and gender, most of which have suggested much hopelessness and despair (and some of which have been elaborated on in this particular book). Ultimately, to ask the question—*to what end* is all this deconstruction needed?—has to be seriously dealt with. Although this final chapter could be judged to be more of the same deconstruction, one of my central points is to elaborate on *alternative* ways to deliberate what social transformation for schools may look like. In some sense, I recount the thoughts and ideas of Cone's opening quotation. His view of freedom is bound within the dialectic of faith and struggle, which is couched within the attempt to both challenge and subsequently undo one's oppression within the social milieu.

Cone's message is indicative of Sharon Welch's (1990) view of how dangerous memories "become dangerous when they are used as the foundation for a critique of existing institutions and ideologies that blur the recognition and denunciation of injustice" (p. 155). Using Martin Luther King as an example, Welch argues that social transformation can and must necessarily start with the existing critique of dominant and oppressive social and cultural structures. For this critique to have any transformative possibilities, these memories and subsequent critiques "must propel people to courageous acts of resistance" (p. 155), while simultaneously never losing a "deep and abiding joy in the wonder of life" (p. 155).

For both Welch and Cone, this joy and hope of transformative possibility is a spiritual reality that challenges oppression, alienation, and subordination. For this purpose I turn to some of liberation theology's central tenets as a stepping stone to what I believe will further the left's emancipatory agenda.

In this chapter, then, I compare and contrast some basic critical pedagogy concepts with liberation theology tenets as a starting point to move to an alternative vision for the educational left.[1] It must

---

[1]In my forthcoming book (Kanpol, in press), I carry the analysis of this chapter further by arguing that an educational left vision must not *only* be grounded in critique, which can at times be cynical, but also be cemented in what I call joy. The interactive dialectic of cynicism and joy represents a moving framework of emancipatory hope that I believe the left has yet to delve into. For a philosophical treatise of "joy" as affirmation as well as a necessary condition for social and political transformation, see Hardt (1993).

be clearly noted that these two paradigms are centered around a transformative consciousness. Their different images around language, metaphors, and symbols, however, are a beginning point to understand how arriving at transformation may be differently surmised. It must also be noted that continued conceptual distinctions between these two forms of language can be viewed by readers as mutually reinforcing and interactive rather than merely dualistic and/or in opposition. My hope is to provide a conclusion that will begin to broaden our view on how we might continue toward a social transformative agenda for the educational left.

Critical Pedagogy Tenets	Liberation Theology Ideals
Language of Possibility	Sense of the Possible
Terrain of Struggle	Sense of the Sacred
Transformative Intellectual	Teacher as Prophet
Group Solidarity	Co-Workers
Border Crossings	Breaking Bread and Talking Back

LANGUAGE OF POSSIBILITY AND SENSE OF THE POSSIBLE

For the critical pedagogist, the *language of possibility* is a term both used and understood for its specific social and cultural transformative possibilities. Simply put, a language of possibility is the beginning point that a teacher uses as a political space to redefine what the classroom may mean in terms of repressing social injustices. This language of possibility will be informed by understanding, searching for, and empathizing with each "owner's" voice, despite the inevitable social and cultural differences that constitute multitudes of voices.

As noted in earlier chapters, in the critical pedagogical tradition, a voice depicts the historical make-up and social experiences of individuals that have been at once alienated, oppressed, and subordinated (McLaren, 1994). A language of possibility allows students and/or teachers to both share and understand their respective voices in light of structural configurations (race, class, gender, age, etc.).

Consequently, one's voice is the stuff that consists of identity. This voice is multifarious. Put simply, one possesses multiple identities concurrently—father, friend, teacher, oppressor, oppressed, authority, authoritarian, lover, and so on. Additionally, the language of possibility presupposes that through understanding one's own and other voice as central to identity, teachers can begin to act as change agents, who, by grasping what constitutes voices, can have a direct impact on altering present oppressive social and cultural conditions. Perhaps put in a more complex way, "voice" also depicts social contradictions, such as elaborated on in Chapters 4 and 5, as well as other areas in this book. For example, a voice of a professor, whose immediate identity can hypothetically be African American and female, has historically been subjugated by race, class, and perhaps gender (Gordon, 1995). This professorial voice now assumes positions of power and authority, despite a history filled with subjugation (West, 1993). In short, this language of possibility seeks to understand such contradictions with the intent to use them as a tool for enlightenment and social transformation.

An alternative to a language of possibility that arises through liberation theology is centered around the notion of *a sense of the possible*. A "sense of the possible" first recognizes the importance of voice for social transformation. Pushed further, a sense of the possible also recognizes that critical pedagogy must be spiritually restorative as well as politically transformative. That is, the human spirit as a desire for being is a spiritual struggle of the most radical order (Kovel, 1991). Human action is constitutive of the soul. Human action in the spiritual sense merges a spirit meaning about the dialectic of self and other and structure and human agency. Unlike a language of possibility, however, within a sense of the possible, a critical pedagogist's struggle is also inherently spiritual, informed by a subject who is at once both inward and expressive, reactive and proactive. Understood a different way, a sense of the possible connotes subjects using the higher powers of one's personal faith, for instance, to search for and elucidate a revolutionary praxis exuding the highest moral and ethical order. It seems to me that this is what helped Freire's (1974) practice (anti-banking and more dialogical teaching strategies, such as critical literacy) as he related his teaching to some Catholic traditions, a method that directly and openly opposes an ideology of social efficiency.

Starting off with Heschel's (1965) basic question of "Who is Man?" (*generic, I believe for male and female*), a sense of the possible presupposes man in partnership with higher powers (in Heschel's case, as a Jew, his convictions for God, or in West's case[2] as a revolutionary Christian, Christ as the son of God), in a struggle over

---

[2]Cornel West's (1982) brilliant analysis of a liberatory struggle based on his faith can be linked to his Marxian analysis of society. For West, prophetic Christianity and social analysis are inseparable. With this in mind, West connects the dialectic of human nature to human history in his discussion of emancipatory possibilities, particularly as related to Black communities.

meaning and living one's life in a morally righteous way. Clearly, Old Testament images of Abraham and Moses and New Testament narratives of Christ historically portray social revolutionaries and the nature of their ethics and spirituality. These human and spiritual beings, as we know, struggled within a society that constantly negated their messages. Resultant beliefs in matter (idols, for instance, in both Abraham's and Moses's case), rather than spirit and/or faith, led people astray. Heschel informs us that man's struggle for justice and peace is in a holy way connected to faith in God as partner in a partisan struggle for a sense of the possible—an ethical, moral, and spiritually restorative order.

I would then agree with Purpel's (1988) basic supposition, written in a recent book review. In short, he claims that the narrative of Jesus, like that of Moses, can serve paradigmatically to help the left overcome critical issues of injustice and other hegemonic oppressive features of our society such as patriarchy. Furthermore, Purpel views these narratives as stories of unconditional love, "an idea that has provoked enormous controversy with extraordinary consequences" (pp. 155-163). It seems to me that both Purpel and Heschel's major thesis is that man's spiritual struggle is a terrain that is sacred, of the holiest order. And although it may seem utopian of me to imagine that the tolerance and/or appreciation of otherness or unconditional love, whether human or nonhuman, will revolutionize our schools, I would agree with Sallie McFague (1993) when she comments:

> It is surely folly to continue to encourage in ourselves and those whom we influence, individualistic, hierarchical, dualistic, and utilitarian ways of thinking that are outmoded and have proved to be destructive of life at all levels. (p. 414)

Given this, there is little doubt that the bridge between the critical language of the left and the spiritual language I am borrowing and developing warrants a theological investigation to similar social and cultural phenomena that have similar ends in mind: social transformation. I now turn to my next distinction.

TERRAIN OF STRUGGLE AND SENSE OF THE SACRED

The notion of "terrain of struggle" is a conceptual lens that critical theorists have previously developed in describing the social and cultural conditions that teachers and other cultural workers face in their daily social transformative agenda's (Aronowitz & Giroux, 1994). The "struggle" is seen as revolving around teachers as cultural reproducers of dominant and stultifying values (or cultural capital involving knowledge, skills, values and attitudes that oppress, alienate and subordinate others) such as excessive competition, rampant individualism and race, class and gender stereotypes, and so on as opposed to active agents in producing alternative conditions for teachers and students (such as cultural capital that challenges oppression, alienation, and subordination).

This terrain of struggle, I argue, is both a cultural and political space. Within this particular struggle, teachers are cultural politicians. With this in mind, as cultural producers, teachers are viewed as counterhegemonic agents, those who challenge and transform dominant and oppressive structures. Their terrain of political and cultural struggle revolves precisely around the morbid, patriarchal, authoritarian, hand-me-down curriculum, social efficiency, and technical mindset that has been historically constructed in schools (Apple, 1986) versus the spaces that teachers create that would challenge and change such a stymied system.

Aronowitz and Giroux argue that to be involved in this struggle means to understand the multiple roles and identities that teachers embody as well as help create in their respective students.[3] These roles and identities are precisely a part of the postmodern condition that Lyotard (1984) theorizes over[4] and what I alluded to earlier as constitutive of voice. Simply put, within this postmodern struggle, in which difference becomes the marker for identity, teachers become the agents of reproduction and production, in flux between the two theoretical and practical areas. They can alienate, subordinate, and oppress while simultaneously possessing the possibility of producing alternative meaning systems that would both challenge and change what schools have historically been constructed for in both a democratic and capitalistic society (Shapiro, 1990).

As a theological construct, the *sense of the sacred* grows out of religious ideals and furthers the argument for the "terrain of struggle" to be broadened. The sacred denotes what is "clean" or acceptable behavior (Purpel, 1989). The New and Old Testament, for instance, attests to particular sacred behaviors, often interpreted in

---

[3]This argument, of course, is related to McLaren's notion of voice, but can be traced back to Freire's use of the dialogical method as a means to unoppress the oppressed.

[4]See Lyotard (1984) for a summary statement on postmodernism. An excellent analysis of the relationship of Lyotard to Education can be seen in a number of essays in Peters (1995).

multiple ways and often related to biblical narratives. Comments hooks (1994):

> I think that ironically, despite all its flaws, religion was one of those places that expanded our our existence. The very fact that in Christian religion Jesus made miracles, well kids growing up in the Christian Church may learn all this other reactionary dogma, but they'll also learn something of an appreciation for mystery and magic. . . . Those biblical stories are fascinating, David and Goliath, Moses parting the Red Sea . . . not only are they fascinating, but they also keep you in touch with the idea that there are forces at work on our lives beyond the world of "reason" and the intellect. So this turning away from religion (in Black culture from traditional black religion) has also meant turning away from a realm of the sacred—a realm of mystery— that has been deeply helpful to us as a people. This is not to say that one only finds a sense of the sacred in traditional Christian faiths. It just seems to be a very tragic loss when we assimilate the values of a technocratic culture that does not acknowledge those higher forms of mystery or even try to make sense of them. (pp. 226-227)

Clearly hooks views the sacred as holy ground, a belief in the mystery of knowledge, the potential to travel beyond the realm of the known into the unchartered waters of the mysterious. Carrying the unknown a little further, I take my cue from Cornel West (1993) and Michael Lerner (1994). I connect the sacred to what West (1993) describes as combative spirituality:

> Combative spirituality sustains persons in their humanity but also transcends solely the political. It embraces a political struggle, but it also deals with issues of death or dread, of despair or disappointment . . . a combative spirituality accents a political struggle but goes beyond it by looking death and dread and despair and disappointment and disease in the face and saying that there is in fact a hope beyond these. (p. 109)

The sense of sacred for West is a belief (as a Christian) that there exists a transcendentalism that guides our personal hopes and dreams. hooks agrees with West here. Coming out of Black history, hooks and West have argued and confessed that Black faith in God is in part a healing process, as well as due to the long traditions of religious faith in the sacred and Black community. Struggle and hardship and authentic belief in the transcendental, they argue, have been countered by a middle-class ideology that has left not only Black America, but also White America in a state of spiritual despair, in which combative spirituality goes begging. Michael Lerner (1994), talking from a Jewish perspective, sees the project of the Jewish people as embracing this sort of combative spirituality. He argues that the Jewish historical project is one of witnessing "the possibility of healing, repair, and transformation of the world, and the rejection of all forms of cynicism and despair" (p. XV111). Lerner also confesses, however, like hooks and West, that mainstream Judaism has assimilated itself so fully into American material life, at the expense of witnessing to others the spiritual messages that the Old Testament delivered. Lerner continues about a contradiction of Modern Judaism:

> In practice, Jewish caring was often limited to caring about Jews. So, as children, they had experienced a community that was giving off two very different messages: one about caring for others; another, often given with greater emotional charge, that we should stop giving to others and worry only about ourselves. (p. 5)

Both West and hooks as well as Lerner point out that nihilism and privilege have robbed the middle class of a social consciousness, a combative spirituality, and a sense of the sacred. hooks and West also argue that along with middle-class status comes responsibility to oneself and the disadvantaged, the obligation of every Jew to give to others who do not have. This brings me back to the sacred as holy and moral territory. The sacred within this framework is about commitment to a life of service, faith and transcendence, to the joy of struggle against the grain of despair and hopelessness (e.g., historically constructed for both Jews and Blacks), simultaneously realizing that although there exists senses of hopelessness, they can only be countered through one's spiritual transcendence.

For the classroom to become a "sacred" and holy place, critical theorists in education must necessarily be involved in the politics of schools and other cultural institutions. Herein lies the "terrain of struggle" initially discussed. Simultaneously, however, this political struggle runs the risk of hopelessness and continual "catch 22" situations (Kanpol, 1988; Willis, 1977) if the struggle is not supported by the kind of political and spiritual message that Martin Luther King ("I have a dream") delivered nearly 30 years ago. This sacred message for teachers connotes that the initial "terrain of struggle" is more than just one that involves cultural reproductive and culturally productive practices of the everyday world, but is also wedded to transcendental hope, belief, and commitment out of hopelessness to the historical, spiritual, and ethical implication of what content and substance it takes to be human (West, 1993), as well as to a belief in the mystery of life that includes the sacred as a departing point for a sense of the possible. It seems to me that the mysterious starts from an intellectual understanding of social and cultural conditions. I argue in the next section that this is not enough for the transformative process.

TRANSFORMATIVE INTELLECTUAL AND TEACHER AS PROPHET

Within the critical theory literature, the term *transformative intellectual* has connoted teacher as a political agent of social change (Giroux, 1988). That is, a transformative intellectual's pedagogical task is to seriously attempt to insert democratic values into all facets of teaching and related activities. This implies taking a stand against teaching for and to a predominant market logic of schools, so well advanced in Bowles and Gintis's (1976) seminal work as well as historically constructed within the American history of education.

Given the schooling and market logic metaphor, exacerbated by national reports (Apple, 1986, especially chap. 6), there lie a number of implications for the transformative intellectual. First, a transformative intellectual will both study and understand the functions of school and surrounding cultural systems, both past and present. An initial understanding of the role of the teacher as socialization agent within the institution of schools is paramount. A deep understanding of race, class, and gender configurations is needed so as to search for ways out of various forms of oppressions. Second, the transformative intellectual will be alert to and act as a change agent from the knowledge, skills, values, and attitudes (cultural capital) set up by the dominant culture within which the school is a part of. Deep structural values such as excessive competition and stereotyping, patriarchal control, mechanistic mindsets, success defined by standardized tests, a survival of the fittest mentality, and so on, all alert the transformative intellectual to the stultifying and oft dehumanizing value structure of schools. Third, the transformative intellectual will set his or her pedagogical task to connect student voices and cultural grammars to multiple sets of realities and differences that constitute multifarious identity. Put differently, in order to unoppress and transform subjugating social relations, fourth, the transformative intellectual must deeply connect and understand the existing borders between his or her narratives and where they belong within the systems value structure and the narratives of different student voices and where they fall prey to oppressive and stultifying values. Fifth, a transformative intellectual will understand the theoretical implications of his or her discourse. Understood another way, a transformative intellectual has the capacity to connect theory to practice, thus inserting politics (values) into all phases of pedagogy. Sixth, and finally, a transformative intellectual takes a decided stance as to what counts as justice and fair play.

That said, a transformative intellectual runs the risk of essentializing his or her democratic values at the expense of students relatavising their values. Thus, the transformative intellectual must weave between creating a pedagogy of dissent from dominant values without essentializing alternative values that can also act as a form of domination. In other words, critical pedagogists as transformative intellectuals run the risk of their zealous commitment acting as final truths, without understanding that the commitment may be a form of essentialism.

Despite this, Giroux and others have been the instigators in a momentous and at times hard-nosed task for critical pedagogists in education. These critical pedagogists are adamant when they speak of the transformative intellectual as a cultural theorist and activist. There is clearly a political agenda for the transformative intellectual, one that transcends the mere classroom as an active area of resistance and transformation, but filters into the dominant culture as well.

I have argued elsewhere that the educational left has often fallen prey to a form of nihilism (see Kanpol, in press; Kanpol & McLaren, 1995). That is, critique for the sake of critique and deconstruction for the sake of deconstruction all too often dominates critical theory discourses in education. What is so empowering about viewing the *teacher as prophet* is that the dialectic of critique and energizing becomes a part of the community of faith committed to altering oppressive social forms. By viewing the teacher as prophet, we can resort to certain biblical figures and narratives as possible social guides to help reconfigure what transformative social agency may look like. For instance, the reality of the exodus from Egypt is the creation of renewed social and cultural possibility. It is the creation or idea and hope of a visionary social community.

Put differently, Moses dismantles the politics of oppression and exploitation by countering it with a politics of justice and compassion (Brueggemann, 1978). Simply, the Israelite flight to salvation was to believe that the undoing of one's own oppression had both spiritual (belief or faith in God and resultant freedom) and cultural (the creation of a new community within a politics of justice) possibilities, and both were mutually reinforcing. The teacher as prophet follows Moses's lead in creating an energizing politics with new realities. Heschel (1962) commented:

> The prophet seldom tells a story, but casts events. He rarely sings, but castigates. He does more than translate reality into a poetic key: he is a preacher whose purpose is not self-expression or the "purgation of emotion" but communication. His images must not shine, they must burn. The prophet is intent on intensifying responsibility, is impatient of excuse, contemptuous of pretense and self-pity. His tone, rarely sweet or caressing, is frequently consoling and disburdening: his words are often slashing, even horrid - designed to shock rather than to edify. . . . The prophet is concerned with wrenching one's conscience from the state of suspended animation. (p. 7)

This quote could be mistaken for a transformative intellectual voice. However, I argue that the teacher as prophet is not only gut-wrenchingly critical of social surroundings, as is a transformative intellectual, but also simultaneously passes on a message of transformative hope, enlightenment, joy and love, and mercy and forgiveness (Purpel, 1988), often left by the wayside within critical educational circles. Unlike the harshly constructed critical language that informs us about the transformative intellectual, the teacher as prophet is concerned with his or her class as sacred and holy ground. Language used must first be critical. Yet, it must also be laced with prophetic and compassionate implications. Such were the lessons taught to us by Jesus, who besides being a leader of unbridled faith, was also daring and active in challenging and undermining the dominant religious traditions of his time, while simultaneously attempting to unoppress the oppressed. Perhaps this Biblical lesson of understanding sin and celebrating joy is a moving dialect of faith that we can all learn from as teachers.[5]

The teacher as prophet will take the joyous lessons learned about cultural transformation and apply them selectively to the classroom. This does not imply that one's religion must intrude or essentialize moral messages. A new community of faith transcends religious barriers. Similarly, teachers as prophets avoid religious essentialism by replacing it faithfully within the dialectics of criticism and joy, nurture and care, and fortitude and grace. Unlike

---

[5]In her brilliant unpublished dissertation, Carol Zinn (1991) argues that faith not only comes from a personal relationship with higher powers such as God, but also is bound within the possibility to confess institutional sin. Her argument places her in a position of conversion that is at once spiritual as much as cultural.

the transformative intellectual whose tradition is built for the most part on nihilistic criticism with a vision for social transformation, the teacher as prophet adds compassion and joy as both a personal emotional reaction to oppressive structures and as public criticism as well as concern about the numbness of the present social context.

Bound within what others have defined as this prophetic tradition is the ultimate responsibility of the teacher as prophet to teach about what it is to be human in a dehumanizing culture. Put in a slightly different way, the teacher as prophet will be responsible to confess to limitations and personal weaknesses, biases, and so on, in the hope to: "celebrate our humanity in all of its aspects—its ugliness as well as its beauty; its animal like as well as it's God-like capacities" (Purpel, 1988, p. 163). As a prophet metaphor, and in more down-to-earth terms, the teacher as an individual transformative intellectual and/or prophet can do little individually to effect social change. I now turn to this issue in this next session.

GROUP SOLIDARITY AND CO-WORKERS

The critical educational literature has been explicit about the need to create group solidarity over transformative praxis both at the university and public school level. Certain studies in education have shown, however, that different forms of group analysis, such as Willis's (1977) Neo-Marxist bent or even my own past poststructural understanding of group solidarity (Kanpol, 1995), is often undermined by capitalistic forms of production. Put differently, often forms of rampant individualism, excessive competition, and a market logic that dominates consciousness undermines attempts by groups of people to effect social and cultural transformation.

I have argued elsewhere that group solidarity analyses can be understood across time and space. That is, struggles to challenge and end various forms of oppression, alienation, and subordination are part of what Laclau and Mouffe (1985) argue to be a democratic imaginary and democratic antagonism, those acts that challenge and suppress areas of alienation, subordination, and oppression. Lacking within the educational left literature are theoretical insights to view how social struggle can and must transcend traditional notions of group solidarity. Clearly, we are not going to get groups of people to strike over issues of teacher and student deskilling and their resultant alienation. This is perhaps evident and evidenced in part by the incessant bombardment of the left's own multifarious political agendas and resultant nonsolidarity (Kanpol & McLaren, 1995).

Clearly, I speak for myself here as well. What we are in need for, however, is an understanding that first there is little hope for group solidarity over transformative issues in the traditional sense. There are too many theoretical and practical blockades that impinge on such a cause. At best, we can hope for various pockets of resistance and solidarity, that in their own capacity act as a "democratic imaginary." This is a good starting point. What the educational left can strive for, then, is a renewed language of hope and possibility, one that is not mired only in nihilistic postmodern analysis, but rather is also constructed around a spiritual lens. With that in mind, I view solidarity efforts by the educational left more as co-workers in a sovereign struggle.

In her work *To Work and To Love: A Theology of Creation*, Dorothee Soelle (1984) points to the need to overcome the traditional split between "God as the Lord, the subject of creation, and the human being as the object, or the stuff of creation made from dust." Soelle argues for a theology that can at once bolster faith in creation while simultaneously viewing creation in a co-worker fashion (God and Human). Put differently, reality is interrelated by events and experiences, for instance, God in Man/Woman. And, although Soelle argues for the permanence in a higher spirit in God, God has the ability to change and be expressive and revealing in a variety of ways.

Such are the arguments, descriptions, and analyses put forth by Lerner (1994) as well. Interesting to note is that Judeo-Christian notions of God differ, yet are bound inextricably by the notion that humans can be viewed as co-creators with God in an effort to overcome selfishness and greed, and both be humbled and uplifted by humility and grace. Such are the images again created by both the Old Testament Moses and the New Testament Jesus, who historically and spiritually struggled politically and with co-workers (Moses with his brother, Aaron, and Joshua, Moses's successor, and Jesus with his disciples) to overcome hopelessness and despair, despite Moses's personal sins, for instance, and all their humanlike suffering. Their messages are both clearly spiritual as well as a social and cultural critique of the times. Their ability to love and to work for justice was profoundly spiritual. They were not merely seeking group solidarity, rather, they were grasping for an existential reality, a vision of the sacred that would win people over in a struggle with and for powers beyond our human control or understanding.

Their relative success is a testimony, not only to both traditions, but also to those who believe in an existential reality as a co-worker metaphor, man/woman with God, one that seeks to combat the oppression of our times. Their actions are reminiscent of seeking a God of eternal and internal power and strength, one who brings

humans together in a mutually empowering co-creative existence. It
is this co-creativity, with and among each other, that potentially
becomes a renewed sense of solidarity. I further this notion in the
next section.

BORDER CROSSINGS AND BREAKING BREAD AND TALKING BACK

In his brilliant recent book *Border Crossings*, prominent critical
educational theorist Henry Giroux (1992) outlines how multiple
theoretical formations inform the everyday world experiences of
subjects. He first argues that a transformative pedagogy is truly
revolutionary if it is able to intersect and not close contradictory
theoretical frameworks of reference. So, for instance, the best of
modernism must intersect with the best of postmodernism, or
feminism's multiple arguments must be viewed within the context of
different racial lines for true borders of understanding between
differences to exist. A border crosser for Giroux is the theorist and/or
practitioner (transformative intellectual) who is able to fluidly both
understand and move between theoretical demarcations spirited by
an emancipatory praxis. Second, for Giroux, a transformative
pedagogy must practice border crossings as part of a cultural politics.
On the even more practical side, some multiculturalists and other
educational theorists (Gordon, 1995) have taken on Giroux's imagery
to depict various cultural understandings of how borders may be
applied to the everyday world.

It is no small claim to make that Giroux has moved
progressive educational theory (various forms of multiculturalists
and critical pedagogists) into the realm of making "difference" far
more intellectually, politically, and practically astute. For years now
critical multiculturalists have dialogued about difference, whether
overtly or covertly, without seriously engaging in the political and
theoretical avenues that Giroux enlightens his readers with. In short,
a multicultural society, according to Giroux, must intertwine borders
of theoretical understandings of the everyday, such as popular
culture (Giroux, 1994; as well as Chapter 8 of this book), as well as
deconstruct one's own culture (in particular, a privileged White
middle-class culture) for true borders to be understood and attained
as well as moved in and through.

Lost within the sophisticated work by Giroux is, perhaps, the
question I alluded to earlier: To what end does one deconstruct for a
border to exist? The end, it could be argued, could be democratic in

intent. However, the kinds of issues Giroux deals with also have to do with the ethical and moral nature of the make-up of each subjectivity. Giroux's message, which catches us in a dialectic of the present state of structural *despair* and the *hope* of a theoretical way out from the gloom and doom, lacks the imagery and subsequent message in which borders of ethics and the moral could also inform critical educational theorists.

In their book *Breaking Bread* (1991), bell hooks and Cornel West take on the imagery of sitting together and critically dialoguing about difference. They come to their readers in a spirit of compassion and solidarity. Comments hooks to West in the introduction of their dialogue, about the vision of testimony of Cone, in which testimony is personal and individual, and in which builds an individual's faith and faith of the community:

> Testimony is a very hard spirit to convey in a written text. . . . It struck me that dialogue was one of the ways where the sense of mutual witness and testimony could be made manifest. I link that sense to regular communion service in the Black church at Yale where we would often stand in a collective circle and sing, "Let us Break Bread Together on Our Knees," and the lines in the song which say, "When I Fall on My Knees with My Face to the Rising Sun, Oh Lord Have Mercy on Me. I liked the combination of the notion of community which is about sharing and breaking bread together, of dialogue as well as mercy because mercy speaks to the need we have for compassion, acceptance, understanding and empathy. (pp. 1-2)

With this image of compassion and breaking bread in mind, important for me is that hooks and West inform readers of the tradition they come from: Black, Christian and believers in God. Breaking bread images "serious talk about coming together, sharing, participating, creating bonds of solidarity . . . linking some sense of faith, religious faith, political faith, to the struggle for freedom" (p. 8).

Breaking bread first brings to mind the image of the Jewish festival of passover, celebrated for Jews in solidarity throughout the world. In breaking the traditional passover bread, Jews are reminded that a central message of passover is one of freedom, hope, and humility in a God that helped free a nation from slavery. Second, the image of breaking break takes me back to Christ in the New Testament. As a Jew, too, he broke bread with his disciples in a bond of solidarity, a common understanding about freedom, in this case, a freedom of and belief in a savior. No matter the interpretation, a simple and profound message is clear. To break bread is to be humble. To "dialogue across difference" (Burbulus & Rice, 1991) is to concede

and understand, incorporate borders of theoretical knowledge into a
common moral and faithful vision for freedom and democracy. To
some, this may mean understanding what Paul's struggle in the new
testament was about—jailed because of his belief's of the highest
moral and faithful order—or what Martin Luther King's message of "I
have a dream" meant, or going back to Romans 1: 2 when connecting
spiritual sides of faith to political transformation:

> And be ye not conformed to this world: but be ye transformed by the
> renewing of your mind.

An appreciation of such transformation may be viewed by
Abraham's rejection of his father's idolatrous life or a deep
appreciation of what sacrifice may have meant as in Abraham's
willingness to sacrifice his son because of belief and conviction to a
higher being. It is as if Abraham, in his rejection of his father's
values, was as bell hooks (1989) described in *Talking Back:*

> Moving from silence into speech is for the oppressed, the colonized,
> the exploited, and those who stand and struggle side by side a
> gesture of defiance that heals, that makes new life and new growth
> possible. It is that act of speech, of "talking back," that is no mere
> gesture of empty words,that is the expression of our movement from
> object to subject—the liberated voice. (p. 9)

It seems to me that images of breaking bread and talking
back can be used as a metaphor by the educational left as a starting
point to understand how we may alternately view social
transformation. It also seems possible that borders of theoretical
understanding can be enhanced with a vision of moral and ethical
responsibility of breaking bread and talking back, one that begins to
answer the question to what end is critical educational theory driven.
Although I do not believe I have provided the answers here, this
chapter has been an initial effort to probe that question, using sparse
Judeo-Christian biblical imagery that seeks a common framework of
reference, despite seeming faith differences. It is also apparent that a
politics of revolutionary hope takes that form of honest commitment,
an example that is again brilliantly and honestly laid out by hooks
and West (1991):

> I remain committed to the prophetic Christian Gospel . . .
> emphasizing the impact of evangelical prophetic Christianity . . .
> rooted in the belief that every individual, irrespective of race, class,
> gender or nationality should have the opportunity of self realization
> and self fulfillment. (p. 22)

It also seems to me that the imagery of Breaking Bread and Talking Back has the potential of creating a dialogue that is guided by a sense of morality and ethics that, as hooks (1991) describes, "takes ones nourishment in the space where you find it" (p. 91), as guided by borders of faith and politics. Clearly, this dialogue means to seriously take Burbules and Rices's (1991) comments up in multiple ways. To dialogue across differences takes on multiple realities. Perhaps, commented West, to dialogue across differences can also mean: "a belief in God that is not to be understood in a non contextual manner. It is understood in relation to a particular context, to specific circumstances (p. 9).

CONCLUSION: SOCIAL TRANSFORMATION AND EPOCHAL TRANSITION

Critical educators who adopt critical pedagogy for *social transformation* need to understand that within multiple theoretical formulations of liberalisms, Marxisms, and feminisms, a sovereign of possibility must be sought as a common good if we are to socially and politically make serious inroads into the dominant culture. I am not suggesting to abandon multiple theoretical formulations as the knowledge construction of regimes of truth. Nor am I saying that all desires, hopes, dreams, and oppressions are totally similar. Equally so, I do agree that all school sites have similar constructs, with similar empowerment, on-site and multicultural agendas. I *am* calling for a form of totalizing vision, however, one that can be likened by the left political faction, particularly in education, to what McLaren (1991) describes as an *epochal transition.*

This transition starts with the postmodern rupture of difference, but becomes, within rupture, a vision of a faith that transcends theoretical discourses without denying their value for *social transformation.* It may lead us toward a higher belief in a spirit that begins to form a community of faith, one that transcends mere similarities and differences of peoples and that also moves into the terrain of what Welch (1990) describes as epistemological solidarity, something she describes as not all too negative:

> An epistemology of solidarity is partial because of its immersion in a particular historical and cultural milieu. It is self-critical because of the recognition that while we are shaped by particular histories, there are other communities affected by us both for good and for ill. Learning from and with those shaped by other equally partial traditions helps avoid sectarianism and totalitarianism. (p. 138)

With this in mind, for the educational left to move theoretically and practically to the kind of transformation I am advocating, once more, the dialectic will have to be negotiated and renegotiated. That is, social transformation and one's faith cannot be viewed as separate. They must be intertwined, feeding off each other, unified within difference and similarity, within and among different traditions, singing the same joyous voice of solidarity in hope and joy. I am not against school prayer, for instance, or even personal (inward) confession or reflection time. Prayer has the possibility of allowing spaces to be critical of one's own material life. At least this is the effect it has on me! To dogmatically take the stance that "we shouldn't have school prayer" is to authoritatively impose oneself on others and/or deny personal "voice," something critical theory in education can do without in the theoretical and practical sense. Thus, school prayer makes sense if contemplation and interpersonal faith is used to understand one's life experiences, be they critical or not.[6]

In this chapter, in particular, I have tried to create theoretical borders with the language of the educational left and some theological visions, as a trend that will be hopefully ongoing with the educational left. It seems to me that border crossings necessarily means to build bridges of faith, similarities, and differences as well as instill ethics into discussion and politics into all phases of our theoretical discourse. Perhaps Kovel (1991) best summarizes how our culture may be fused with spirituality when he calls for a new sense of the possible within a radically spiritual attitude, one that Purpel (1989) so eloquently describes as "whose sense of education can be seen to be critical, in that its purpose is to help us to see, hear and experience the world more completely, and with more understanding" (p. 126). It is here that critical pedagogy and liberation theology offers the educational left as a necessary border for the transformative agenda, particularly as we commonly struggle to search for boundaries of human hope and possibility.

---

[6]In my mind the struggle over school prayer is one that the left has to use to its advantage. In other words, how we use the common and "affective" language that mobilizes popular opinion is the terrain the Left has to deal with in order to enhance its political/cultural cause. For me, and particularly my students, I use the language of the religious right in order to redefine how this language may be constitutive of different and hopefully critical and visionary spiritual realities.

1. How is your particular faith connected to social action?
   a. Is having a faith necessary for social action? Why or why not?
2. What future short- and long-term trends do you see for critical pedagogy?
3. What in critical pedagogy can you apply to your everyday world both in and out of the classroom?
4. How would you justify critical pedagogy as an alternative to social efficiency, particularly to a beginning teacher or a teacher in the field who is stagnated within this social efficiency mindset?
5. Is critical pedagogy in many or some of its aspects a feasible alternative to social efficiency as an educational philosophy?
6. Where can you use critical pedagogy?
7. If you had to describe critical pedagogy to a would-be teacher, what would you say? Justify your response.

REFERENCES

Apple, M. (1986). *Teachers & texts*. New York: Routledge.

Aronowitz, S., & Giroux, H. (1994). *Education still under siege*. Westport, CT: Bergin & Garvey.

Bowles, S., & Gintis, H. (1976). *Schooling in capitalist America*. New York: Basic Books.

Brueggemann, W. (1978). *The prophetic imagination*. Philadelphia: Fortress Press.

Burbulus, N., & Rice, S. (1991). Dialogue across difference: Continuing the conversation. *Harvard Educational Review, 61*(4), 393-416.

Cone, J. (1986). *Speaking the truth: Edumenism, liberation and Black theology*. Grand Rapids, MI: W. B. Eerdmans.

Freire, P. (1974). *Pedagogy of the oppressed*. New York: Seabury Press.

Giroux, H. (1988). *Teachers as intellectuals: A critical pedagogy for practical learning*. Westport, CT: Bergin & Garvey.

Giroux, H. (1992). *Border crossings*. New York: Routledge.

Giroux, H. (1994). *Disturbing pleasures*. New York: Routledge.

Gordon, B. (1995). The fringe dwellers: Afro-American women in the postmodern era. In B. Kanpol and P. McLaren (Eds.), *Critical multiculturalism: Uncommon voices in a common struggle* (pp. 59-88). Westport, CT: Bergin & Garvey.

Hardt, M. (1993). *Giles deleuze.* Minneapolis: University of Minnesota Press.

Heschel, A. (1965). *Who is man?* Stanford, CA: Stanford University Press.

Heschel, A. (1962). *The prophets* (2nd vol.). New York: Harper & Row.

hooks, b. (1994). *Outlaw culture: Resisting representation.* New York: Routledge.

hooks, b., & West, C. (1991). *Breaking bread.* Boston: South End Press.

hooks, b. (1989). *Talking back: Thinking feminist, thinking Black.* Boston: South End Press.

Kanpol, B. (1988). Teacher work tasks as resistance and accommodation to structural factors of schools. *Urban Education, 23*(2), 173-187.

Kanpol, B. (1992). *Towards a theory and practice of teacher cultural politics: Continuing the postmodern debate.* Norwood, NJ: Ablex.

Kanpol, B. (1995). Multiculturalism and empathy: Towards a border pedagogy of solidarity. In B. Kanpol & P. McLaren (Eds.), *Critical multiculturalism: Uncommon voices in a common struggle* (pp. 177-196). Westport, CT: Bergin & Garvey.

Kanpol, B. (in press). *Teachers talking back and breaking bread.* Cresskill, NJ: Hampton Press..

Kanpol, B., & McLaren, P. (1995). *Critical multiculturalism: Uncommon voices in a common struggle.* Westport, CT: Bergin & Garvey.

Kovel, J. (1991). *History and spirituality: An inquiry into the philosophy of liberation.* Boston: Beacon Press.

Kozol, J. (1991). *Savage inequalities.* New York: Crown.

Laclau, E., & Mouffe, C. (1985). *Hegemony and socialist strategy.* London: Verso.

Lerner, M. (1994). *Jewish renewal.* New York: Putnam.

Lyotard, J. F. (1984). *The postmodern condition.* Minneapolis: University of Minnesota Press.

McFague, S. (1993). A new sensibility. In S. Shapiro & D. Purpel (Eds.), *Critical social issues in American education* (pp. 408-428). New York: Longman.

McLaren, P. (1991). Schooling and the postmodern body: Critical pedagogy and the politics of enfleshment. *Journal of Education, 170*(3): 53-83.

McLaren, P. (1994). *Life in schools*. New York: Longman.

Peters, M. (1994). *Education and the postmodern condition*. Westport, CT: Bergin & Garvey.

Purpel, D. (1988). Review article: Schooling as a Ritual Performance. *Educational Theory, 38*(1), 155-163.

Purpel, D. (1989). *The moral and spiritual crisis in education*. Westport, CT: Begin & Garvey.

Shapiro, S. (1990). *Between capitalism and democracy*. Westport, CT: Bergin & Garvey.

Soelle, D. (1984). *To work and to love: A theology of creation* Philadelphia: Fortress Press.

Welch, S. (1990). *A feminist ethic of risk*. Minneapolis: Fortress Press.

West, C. (1982). *Prophesy deliverance: An African-American revolutionary christianity*. Philadelphia: Westminster Press.

West, C. (1993). *Prophetic reflections*. Monroe, ME: Common Courage Press.

Willis, P. (1977). *Learning to labor*. Lexington: D.C. Heath.

Zinn, C. (1991). *Teaching as a religious activity: The classroom as a place of darkness and mystery*. Unpublished doctoral dissertation, University of North Carolina at Greensboro.

Author Index

A

Adams, W., 72, 75, 77
Altenbaugh, R., 41, *44*
Anyon, J., 7, *17*, 38, *44*, 51, 59, *62*, 131, 132, *145*
Apple, M., 3, 7, *17*, 34, *44*, 59, *62*, 67, 77, 130, *145*, 152, 155, *165*
Aronowitz, S., 36, 39, *44*, 55, 60, *62*, 68, 77, 152, *165*
Ashendon, D.J., 67, 77
Associated Press, 12, *17*

B

Bailey, G., 72, 75, 77
Bakan, D., 68, 77
Banks, J., xii, 52, *62*
Bergessen, A., 39, *44*
Beyer, L., 70, 77
Boateng, F., 105, *112*
Bowles, S. 7, *18*, 155, *165*
Britzman, D., 59, *62*, 118, *128*, 132, *145*

B

Brueggemann, W., 156, *165*
Bullough, R., Jr., 34, 36, 39, *44*
Burbules, N., 95, 96, 98, 107, *112*, 131, *145*, 162, 163, *165*

C

Capper, C., 3, *18*, 134, 135, 137, *145*
Carlson, D., 41, *44*, 100, *112*
Comer, J., 99, *112*
Cone, J., 30, *32*, 147, *165*
Connell, R.W., 67, 77
Daly, W., 68, 77
Darder, A., 5, 14, *18*, 52, *62*, 95, *112*
Dewey, J., 7, 8, *18*, 90, *91*
Dodson-Grey, E., 68, 77
Dowsett, G.W., 67, 77

E

Ellsworth, E., 12, 14, *18*, 75, 77, 133, *145*
Everhart, R., 34, *44*

169

Subject Index